To

I hope [illegible] is well with the IT world. Best wishes

EXPERT PERFORMANCE

ACHIEVE EXTRAORDINARY RESULTS WITH THE TEAM YOU HAVE -- GUARANTEED!

Dr. Vince Racioppo

Published 2019
Printed in the United States of America

Print ISBN: 978-0-578-60005-5
Publisher Information:

RHG Media Productions
25495 Southwick Drive #103
Hayward, CA 94544

www.YourPurposeDrivenPractice.com

CONTENTS

ACKNOWLEDGEMENTS

With great appreciation, I thank my wife Barbara, whose unwavering support sustains me and lifts me up to be my best. She has been my true North Star, lighting my way to become all I can be. I wish to express gratitude for my very special friend and coach, Sarah Victory, who has offered a steady hand, offering endless encouragement and helping me realize the greatness I have within. She is a very special person whose untiring optimism helped me hone my gifts and help me to realize, "I can do this!". A special place in my heart belongs to my friend and colleague, Ann Clancy, who began the journey with me when this book was merely a thought. She encouraged, always focused on my strengths, and held up a mirror for me to see the best of myself. My thanks extends to my friends at Weaver Consultants Group, particularly Doug Dorgan, Jeff Young, and John Weaver, whose shining example taught me about the value of compassionate and caring leadership.

Finally, to my dear friend David Massello, whose towering creativity and intellect has stretched my thinking and helped me to become a better writer, coach, speaker, and consultant. I am grateful that we walk the same path.

SEE WHAT PEOPLE ARE SAYING ABOUT *EXPERT PERFORMANCE*

"Simply put...one of the best business books in my reading history."
Tom Walter, Owner and Chief Cultural Officer, Tasty Catering

"Read this book immediately! In his powerful new book, Vince Racioppo will help you to instantly be more successful as a leader, and make your team ten times more effective."
Sarah Victory, best-selling author and award-winning speaker, President, Victory Company

"I've read lots of books on leadership and *Expert Performance* is one of the best!"
Olivia Parr-Rud, MS, Expert Data Scientist, Corporate Love Ambassador, Self-Love Advocate, Olivia Group

"Vince has created a rich blend of leadership development and coaching experience supported by a vast array of tools and activities to take the guesswork out of becoming a top-notch leader. This book is truly interactive and insightful for us all."
Linda F. Patten, Leadership Trainer for Women Entrepreneurs and Changemakers.
President &CEO, Dare2Lead With Linda

"When it comes to understanding what motivates and inspires your most valuable resource, your team, this book is your go-to guide. *Expert Performance* is packed with best-in-class strategies that you can use for positive results right away."
Wendy Benson, 2x2 Health: Private Health Concierge

"Fantastic read!!! Full of great ideas to identify your organization's "Powerful Purpose" and to develop your team."
Jeff Young, Co-President, Weaver Consultants Group

“Whether you are leading a small project team or a large corporation, there are insights and practical leadership skills that will bring a new perspective on your historical approach to leadership.”

Douglas Dorgan, Co-President, Weaver Consultants Group

FOREWORD

Vince is one of those "shining leaders" that he talks about in his book. He has focused on a deeper understanding and application of **expert performance** all of his professional career and lives or embodies the skills, the practices, and the level of mastery and awareness that is needed to help others achieve expert performance.

One of Vince's signature strengths is establishing relationships. When he meets with his clients and they begin to talk about their situation, without conscious awareness on his part, he builds his clients up, raises their awareness about their capabilities, and encourages their success—all in an absolutely sincere and grounded way. Vince simply cannot NOT interact with his clients in this way; it is his coaching and consulting stance, as he genuinely believes in the capabilities of every client he meets.

I first met Vince in a coaching capacity, as he wished to learn more about a positive or generative way of coaching his clients rather than a deficit, problem-solving approach. This became clear to me once we started working together. Of course! Vince is incapable of working without care, compassion, and sheer joy in helping people, teams, and organizations be the best they can be. Since this is so much a part of who Vince is, his book brings to readers his accumulated research, experience, collaborative efforts, deep beliefs, and sheer strength in showing others their capabilities and potential.

With this book, Vince presents a practical, evidence-based practice for those readers interested, even compelled, to learn concrete ways to become expert leaders in or for their organizations. He provides a step-by-step process, creating a clear path forward that builds on one component after another to showcase a comprehensive "how-to" guide. As he so clearly states in his introduction, his book takes the guesswork out of becoming a performance expert with his focus on deliberate practice.

He has chapters covering ways to incorporate expert performance into hiring, training, engaging, and growing employees. He describes the significance of setting up profitable systems and processes and of harnessing the power of influencing as skills essential to cultivating top performance. He also provides excellent guidance on building expert team performance, including "fostering amazing decision-making" and five ways to find the "bright shining stars" in people.

As an Organization Development consultant, strategic planner, and executive coach, I found his book to encompass the breadth, depth, and simplicity necessary to truly help leaders capitalize on their unique strengths. In reading his book, Vince will become your coach, supporting you in applying the strategies and practices he has collected to bring expert performance into organizations. It is well researched and grounded in his own, and others', lived practice and experience.

Over the years, I have gotten to know Vince as a husband, father, friend and colleague. It would be remiss of me not to highlight how congruent Vince is in his personal and professional lives. He is one of those gifted individuals, if you are lucky enough to work with him, where what you see is what you get. He is the very essence of what he is conveying in this book. He is a ceaseless learner, curious and caring about what he focuses his attention on and, above all else, an individual who truly loves to work with others for the betterment of all. You will feel the spirit of Vince in this writing as he reaches out to you, the reader, and you will discover yourself fully engaged!

Ann L. Clancy, Ph.D.
Clancy Consultants, Inc.
Appreciative Coaching Collaborative, LLC.
Co-author of *Pivoting: A Coach's Guide to Igniting Substantial Change*, 2017
Co-author of *Appreciative Coaching: A Positive Process for Change*, 2007

CHAPTER 1

INTRODUCTION

Set out on the journey to become extraordinary

Imagine being the shining leader that everyone wants to work for, the person who gets results, hires the best, and creates a culture that is the envy of others. This book shares the secrets of that magic. It is the culmination of over twenty years of consultation and research containing inspirational examples and interviews with people who have succeeded. This book will change the way you lead and bring out the very best in you.

Insider Secrets That Make You an Expert Leader

In this book, you will discover the hidden secrets that will help you become an expert leader. If you want to be a doctor, an airline pilot, an electrician or plumber, someone more skilled than you would apprentice you, showing you the ropes. That expert would guide you and develop you to become an expert in your own right. You would master the activities that increased your abilities until you became extraordinary at your craft.

Many leaders, particularly those in small to midsize organizations, don't have someone of outstanding capabilities to teach them, nor do they know the behaviors to practice. Most of the time they're guessing, and if they get lucky, their leadership improves.

I'm reminded of my days in Little League baseball. We thought the best way to become better as players was to watch major league athletes. We became adept at imitation. We could expertly dig with our shoes, spit, and scratch with the best of them, none of which helped us become better players. Later I learned that the best athletes fully understand the game, other player capabilities, and the game strategies, all of which made them successful. Without this understanding of how people think then behave, our dreams of becoming major league baseball players drifted away. Leaders struggle with the same issues. There is little that one can study or learn to become the very best. Up to now, there have been no step-by-step best practices that leaders could follow to become expert performers in their field.

After my corporate career, successful consulting projects, and hundreds of interviews over a 22-year career, I have distilled the capabilities that create expertise and high performance.

This book takes the guesswork out of becoming a top-notch leader.

We know from research (Anders Ericsson, Richard Poole, *Peak: Secrets from the New Science of Expertise*, Houghton Mifflin, 2016) that becoming an expert requires deliberate practice that stretches, grows, and challenges us to increase our abilities daily. Experience will not necessarily make you an expert leader. As a pianist, for example, it's not good enough to practice daily the same song learned two years ago. There is no stretch or growth, which is precisely what we need to increase our abilities.

Deliberate practice requires another element–practice must lead to improvement. For example, I can hit a bucket of balls at the golfing range and get very good at being very bad, with my bad habits continuing to haunt me. I practice, then perfect, an already bad slice! Without correction from a coach, we drift from one bad habit to another. With a coach, we receive the feedback that points us in the direction of excellence.

This book acts as that coach, providing you, as a leader, the skills that, when practiced regularly and deliberately, will grow your expert performance.

In one of my early engagements, I studied the expertise of high-performing salespeople then taught that expertise to others. The results were profoundly surprising. Within a short time, ninety days, the sales group who learned the techniques of top performers increased their sales by an average of nearly 40%. One person even doubled his sales. I learned a valuable lesson from this engagement. If someone wants to become an expert, that person must practice in the same way that experts perform. If you practice the behaviors in this book, you can become an expert leader also.

Most of us have experienced expert leaders. These are the people who provide organizations with extraordinary guidance through storms and challenges, who focus their teams to produce results at levels greater than 90% of their peers. They powerfully influence others, moving entire companies forward towards success. They create high levels of loyalty and following, enabling their teams to work in concert to achieve seemingly impossible results. Their compassion, understanding, and care reverberate through their businesses, attracting high-performing talent, creating an inviting and embracing workplace, and making their workplace THE company where everyone wants to work. These leaders create no jealousy or envy, always lending a helping hand to elevate everyone around them to success.

Every chapter presents an opportunity for growth so that you too will become expert leader. At the end of each chapter, you'll find opportunities to stretch yourself, opportunities that provide you with deliberate practice.

Expert Leaders Care

When I was a young boy, I hated to run errands with my father in my hometown of New Castle, Pennsylvania. By the time I was 10, my father had been teaching ninth-grade science at the Ben Franklin Junior High School for over thirty years. Without fail, each trip with Dad meant running into a former student who wanted to talk for what seemed to me to be an eternity. What should have been a thirty-minute trip usually turned into an hour or more.

Like many kids, I inadvertently gained a lesson that I only recently learned to value. With each of his former students, Dad would listen patiently as they recalled their life since the two had last seen each other. He would ask questions, always showing sincere, deep interest and concern for the ins and outs of his pupils' lives. I, of course, registered increasing impatience, asking my dad if we could move on. He would acknowledge me, ask a few more questions of his student, then we would continue with our mission, which had started as something to do with buying food and ended up with meeting others whom he knew.

Many of the former students who would stop him on the street would tell him what an extraordinary teacher he was: "You changed my life" or "Because of you, I found a life's career."

Once, we heard of a story of a woman missionary who had spoken to a congregation. She talked about a teacher she had in junior high school who told her to always reach for the fruit highest on the tree, for there it is the sweetest. She had lived her life with that in mind. That teacher was my father.

I, unfortunately, never had the opportunity to sit in his class since I went to a different school. Ironically, my mother-in-law had my dad for class, as did several of my aunts and my mother's cousins. Every one of these people told me what an excellent teacher my father was. Many did not remember one single piece of science, but they recalled his life lessons, his caring, his compassion, and his enthusiastic support of them as people. Late in his career, the school asked him to teach seventh-grade math. My father would come home from work distressed at how unprepared students were. The children had been passed on to the next grade even though they failed at the simplest age-appropriate math. My father could have taken the easy route, passing them on to the next level, but rather than let the children fail, he worked diligently to catch them up so that they might succeed.

When he passed away at age 89, at his funeral, many of his former students, now middle-aged and older, told me how he had changed their lives. Each recounted their personal story of my Dad listening, supporting, and encouraging. What more could one want from one's life than to be remembered in that way?

My father was an expert teacher, an expert performer who did what I have discovered expert leaders do. They care, have compassion, and a willingness to help anyone willing to try. Join other top leaders, leaving a legacy that has made a tremendous difference in other's lives.

Insider Information You Will Discover

The first three chapters, "Hire the Best," "Train for Success," and "Engage and Grow Your Employees," explain the behaviors expert leaders use to staff and engage people to become the very best possible. The next chapter, "Your Hidden Strengths," contains a discussion of a discovery I made while working with and interviewing top leaders. These experts have a strong understanding of their strengths, maximizing these strengths by working on them every day.

The chapter titled "Be More Profitable" will help leaders to understand the importance of teaching employees how a company makes money, specifically how employees add to the revenue and profit of their organization. With minimal exceptions, I have found that employees want to contribute, particularly when it means increasing the bottom line. As leaders move up into their organizations, the next chapter, called "How to Lead Leaders," explains the expertise that top performers use to help reporting managers to succeed.

I have found that the very best leaders have tremendous skills in influencing others, so the next chapter, "The Power of Influence," is one you will want to pay particular time studying and reading. If you don't know where to begin on your leadership journey, then this chapter is the perfect place to start.

For those leaders who want to expand expertise in their organization, the chapter titled "How to Get Top Performance" explains the techniques that I use to uncover expertise of the very best. You can use these techniques to identify high-performance behaviors in your organization and then teach others these powerful behaviors.

The next to last chapter, called "Build Your Expert Performance Team," discusses six behaviors leaders can use to help their teams become incredibly high functioning. Expert leaders create top-notch, A-level teams.

The last chapter, called "Finding the Bright Shining Star," presents five different ways to bring out the best in employees. The section explains the means to create an environment in which people perform at their best.

How to Use This Book

Since every chapter provides opportunities for practice, choose the areas in which you would like to grow and develop. Find the chapters that offer you the most opportunity to stretch yourself and grow new behaviors. My goal is to help you become the very best.

CHAPTER 2

HIRE THE BEST

The secrets for hiring top people who deliver results

How many times has your organization hired someone who they thought to be top-notch, only to see them fail within a short time? High-performance employees and teams drive the success of any organization. Hiring is the gateway to creating an organization that soars. If you get hiring right, many of the issues and problems your organization may face will dissolve.

Hiring is a challenging process that most organizations do not do well and relegate it to a recruiter in human resources who may not fully understand the nuances of the business.

Even more disconcerting, hiring mistakes are expensive. One organization with whom I worked invested the equivalent of a year's salary in each one of their project managers. Losing a person (and they lost plenty) cost them their investment. Fast Company writes that 27% of US employers surveyed said that just one bad hire costs their company more than $50,000. Hiring poor salespeople dramatically increases exposure. Brad Smart, in his book, *Top Grading*, notes from his surveys that failure of top sales employees can reach into the nine figures, particularly when one includes lost opportunity costs. These costs are imbedded and invisible, scattered across your profit and loss statement, ultimately decreasing your bottom line.

Why does hiring fail?

- Hiring managers frequently do not know the details of the job for which they are hiring. For example, one of my clients is the CEO of a small manufacturing organization, and he wants to hire a controller, a position he has never held.
- Frequently, job descriptions are not written in sufficient detail to enable recruiters and other interviewers (including hiring managers)

to determine whether the candidate fully meets the needs of the organization. Later in this chapter, I will help you define the competency categories which we have found make the most difference in employee performance.

- Budgets require us to hire well below the competency level needed for the job. Unfortunately, many individuals who we hire at a lower capability level never receive sufficient training and development to reach the desired competency level and eventually fail.

- Finally, hiring managers hire infrequently. To become fully proficient at hiring requires understanding and practice. Most hiring managers do not have the background and skill necessary to conduct best-in-class interviews.

Hiring can fail even when we bring on someone we believe is the right person for the job, but after onboarding, the position responsibilities shift from the original intentions because of other, more pressing business needs. Here is a real life example.

Eileen walked in the door of Jim's (the CEO's) office. Eileen appeared to be a great candidate for the HR Director position, and Jim was excited to think he might have Eileen on his team. During the interviews, her bright, energetic personality quickly won over the interviewing managers. Jim thought to himself, "What a great find. We're lucky to have her apply here."

Someone like Eileen was important to Jim. For the last several years, he had felt dissatisfaction that the culture of his electronics manufacturing plant seemed harsh and unfeeling. His previous efforts to shift the environment to greater compassion had failed, and now he sought someone whose nature would inspire change. From his interview, he felt strongly that Eileen's personal traits would lead to a positive and dramatic transformation, creating the kind of culture that would engage his plant employees. He wanted her to lead the effort that would make Jim's company the place everyone wanted to work.

All began well. Just as Eileen had connected with the interview team, she built strong relationships to the plant management. People liked her and trusted her. They asked her for advice. She helped managers soften their approach, and the team could see the results immediately. But in the background, years of a tough culture had taken a toll, causing turnover to soar. Jim had no choice but to have Eileen turn her exclusive attention to increasing staffing, a discipline that was not her strong suit.

Recruiters are specialists who spend their days finding top-notch candidates for their organizations. Unfortunately, finding employees takes capabilities and skills that Eileen did not have in her job skillset.

Eileen's shifting priorities and shortage of qualified staff closed the door on her cultural change work, and the effort fell by the wayside. Even worse for Eileen, she failed to keep up with the staffing needs of the organization. To Jim, she appeared to lack success in both aspects of her job.

Unfortunately, as time passed, Eileen's performance fell further behind. Managers complained that inadequate staffing slowed manufacturing throughput, affecting the plant's profitability. As pressure to produce escalated, the culture returned to its rougher state.

In Jim's mind, Eileen, who had showed so much promise, failed completely. After such a great start, regrettably, Jim had to let Eileen go.

Jim was right to question himself, asking, "Where did I fail on this hire? How did I not see the signs? How could I do better in the future?" Jim was correct in trying to improve his culture, but he did not understand how severely his poor enviornment had impacted staffing.

How to Hire the Best

Great companies begin by clearly defining the job for which they are hiring. The individual must be fully competent to do the job, or the company has the resources available to bring the person up to full competency level.

We want to reduce the role of chance in hiring. Having the following competencies defined clearly assures that we take a scientific approach to improve our odds of hiring top people. When we can break our competencies into detailed subgroups, we dramatically increase our chances of successful hiring. Most organizations do a proficient job at defining the knowledge, skills, and experience a candidate must have to succeed. However, for a typical position, these three elements make up less than half the attributes that create success and high performance. Further, our decision making can be confused by other less-contributory factors that prevent us from a more objective decision.

These less important factors can further impede good selection. Unconscious feelings of trust can skew our selection process as it does with product and service selection. For example, Daniel Kahneman discovered that individuals would instead do business with a person they like and trust rather than someone they do not, even if the other person offers a product or service at a lower price. When applied to hiring, managers may experience a gut feeling of trust connection, that, without objective information, may create misalignment with fact.

From my experience, the most effective job descriptions contain the following elements that, when combined, create a robust framework for hiring the best.

- **Tasks** – Tasks are the core of a job description, allowing us to specify the duties and activities a person must perform. Generally, most organizations get this right about 80 to 90% of the time. We can fail to produce an adequate task list if we do not understand the job. For example, we may not understand higher-level positions such as controllers or executives, and we, therefore, fail to capture the nuances of these jobs. To obtain the details of positions may require observation of either incumbents or of those performing a similar function.

- **Knowledge** – Candidates must have a minimal level of job knowledge. If we have to teach our new hires the basics, but we don't have the resources to do so, we put the outcomes of the organization in jeopardy.

- **Skills** – Successful candidates must have necessary skill levels, such as the ability to make complex calculations or use a spreadsheet. Ordinarily, organizations are quite good at specifying the required skills and knowledge.

- **Experience** – The experience of the candidate may add significant reasons for success. Experience, as in on-the-job training, brings individuals a leg up on those who have limited time in the position. Many organizations specify the number of years of experience. I have found these to be somewhat arbitrary and do not recommend you use an exact number as a filter for identifying unqualified candidates. Two years of experience in a major accounting firm may have a far more significant impact than two years at a small, boutique company.

  I have observed two common errors when defining knowledge, skills, and experience.

The first error is a lack of clear understanding of the knowledge, skills, and experience necessary to do the job. This error is more likely to occur when the individual who is hiring has not performed in the position.

The second and more common error occurs when our budgets prevent us from hiring a person of sufficient competency levels.

One of my clients had to hire four new individuals for his department. His performance plan requires him to maintain a 70% billable rate in the consulting firm, i.e., he needs to bill 70% of his time to clients. Unfortunately, the four people he hired, through no fault of their own, were not up to full competency level for the job. He, therefore, had to spend much of his time teaching and training, and, consequently, his billable rate fell to 50%.

He was expected to make up that 20% difference by working extra hours. Such overtime hours can lead to fatigue, burnout, and attrition. Unfortunately, the majority of organizations failed to capture the cost of developing and training people to full capability levels.

- **Cultural fit** – As you know, every organization has a distinctive culture. During my days in IBM, when we hired someone who functioned outside our culture, the organizational immune system activated, and the individual realizing the bad fit departed quickly. Strong cultures can have a profound effect on how well an individual performs.

  We think of culture as having three components that are all necessary for an organization's high performance. First, the culture has to focus on high customer satisfaction levels with people in the organization feeling driven to exceed customer needs. Second, the organization must establish a highly focused effort to engage employees. In high-performing cultures, these employees willingly bring discretionary effort to the workplace, offering their talents, thoughts, and creativity to advance the organization. Third, organizations must have tight financial controls. The most effective organizations we see are those that share financial information with their employees, creating a sense of camaraderie and collaboration as these employees work to reach business goals.

- **Learning ability** – Our research tells us that our ability to learn is one of the single most significant factors that contribute to an individual's work success. I am reminded of an individual who I helped to hire at a company with whom I was working. Others liked this individual, and we believed he had all the characteristics necessary to perform at a high level. Unfortunately, the individual could not work with spreadsheets, a critical component of his job. Even after multiple interventions and training, he remained unable to master these essential tools. As a result, the company was forced to let this individual go.

- **Ability to work in a team** – More and more, work funnels through teams who often out-produce individual effort. Organizations continue to drive out bureaucracy and, with that, layers of management. Companies no longer can afford to have top-down, command-and-control leadership since many individuals in today's workforce will not tolerate this kind of leadership.

- **Emotional intelligence** – Our ability to work cooperatively with and influence others has a profound impact on the success of our organization. Emotional intelligence predicts success in the workplace, particularly as leaders ascend in their careers. Interestingly, in opposition to cognitive intelligence, emotional intelligence can be learned and continues to grow into our 60s, when most people retire from their organizations. When hiring, we can screen for emotional intelligence with the understanding that those who score less than competency level can be developed and trained to increase their EI. I use the EQ-I 2.0 and EQ 360, which can be found at www.mhs.com (look under talent offerings).

Below is an example of a simple job description. As job complexity increases, the job description becomes more detailed. As you can see, a good job description requires considerable effort, but the payoff can be enormous. From the brief job description below, the cost to move someone from hiring to full capability will need the organization to expand $37,000. Bear in mind that each unsuccessful hire wastes those development efforts, costing the organization the entire $37,000. Note that the $37,000 does not include any lost opportunity costs, which, if included, could increase the employee loss to six figures.

	Detailed description of minimal competency for hiring	Detailed description when at a competency level	How will the person be brought up to competency level	Estimated cost description	
Knowledge	Has completed the coursework for an accounting degree	Knowledge of our internal accounting practices.	Will connect individual to a senior accountant who will teach the required practices.	120 hours of senior accountants time over one year.	$6,000
Skills	Must know how to use Excel basics	Must be able to create Pivot tables from raw data including averages and sums.	Will send the individual to course on Excel. Will have the individual use Excel Pivotables	Excel course and work with senior accountant	$500
Experience	One year working at a 100 person or more accounting firm	One additional year working at our firm	Teach the following: 1) How to conduct a month-end closing. 2) Produce job-costing reports for your assigned team.	Lowered productivity calculated at 1/3 salary	$20,000
Cultural Fit	Has worked In teams in previous jobs and college. Is assertive but not demanding.	Has excellent client service. Understands company financials. Works well within our teams.	Learn the mission and vision of our organization. Place on an internal team. Review company financials with the individual.	Lowered productivity of internal team.	10,000
Learning Ability	Has an IQ of at least 110. Has a drive to learn new things.	n/a	n/a	n/a	n/a
Ability to work in a team	Treats all people with dignity and respect.	Treats all people with dignity and respect. Willing to do what is necessary to get the job done, i.e. has drive	Teach about drive and expectations for performance.	Included above	Included above

Emotional Intelligence	Scores in the top 20% of emotional intelligence instruments	Scores in top 10% of emotional intelligence instruments	Develop emotional intelligence through use of online learning	Subscription to online emotional intelligence learning	500
Investment to bring person to competency level					$37,000

Find the Candidates Using Artificial Intelligence

One of my clients has recognized an opportunity in the marketplace for high-quality plumbing and HVAC services. Sometimes customers find it challenging to get good people to come to their homes or businesses to make repairs. Filling this service vacuum creates significant financial upsides if we can find the people who have plumbing and HVAC licenses.

Herein lies the problem. The organization found only one individual applying each month, but they want to add fifty new licensed individuals. The existing slow four-year employee acquisition curve would not meet the financial strategies of the company.

Enter the world of artificial intelligence. The client engaged a company whose artificial intelligence engine searches the Internet for hidden passive licensed individuals. Once found, the artificial intelligence program engages the individual in a natural-language conversation to determine whether the person would be a good match for the client. Recently, the client was able to bring on board four licensed individuals in just a few weeks.

Artificial intelligence is changing the way we find candidates. Other applications that run on smartphones can now compare your experiences to any job on the Internet and make matches. Job boards and postings will gradually become less and less critical.

Artificial intelligence chatbots engage potential candidates in natural-language conversations. When a candidate inquires about a job, the chatbot determines whether the individual qualifies for the position, all without human intervention. Once the candidate is qualified, a human completes the screening process.

We can even turn scheduling over to artificial intelligence. I use X.AI, which looks at my calendar then offers dates and times for those with whom I want to connect, all done through natural-language processing.

Assessments

Just a note of caution on the use of assessments. If you're using a homegrown assessment, show statistical evidence that the assessment predicts job performance. Otherwise, you open yourself up to unfair hiring practices and potential lawsuits. If you are using other measurements, assure yourself that the tools are valid, and predict success in the job. Many tools, such as the DiSC, are ipsative, that is they are based on a self-assessment and are not predictive of performance on the job. These tools are not defensible, so if a candidate files a lawsuit, you would be unable to defend the use of such an instrument. Check the norming process for the instrument, making sure it has been normed across a large population and indeed does predict outcomes.

Homegrown assessments:

One of the most underused tool groups used for hiring is assessments. One of my clients was interviewing for an engineering consulting position. The two candidates, I'll call Joe and Denise, both presented well during interviews. The consensus was that, of the two, Joe had the most outgoing and engaging personality. His verbal communication skills were excellent, and the hiring team thought he would be a definite asset to the organization. Recently, as part of the hiring process, the organization decided to implement a real-life assessment consisting of a typical client problem. The candidate then is to spend 45 minutes offering written recommendations. The results came back counter to what they anticipated. Denise had more precise, consistent, and creative responses in comparison to Joe's, whose writing and thought processes were substandard. Subsequently, the firm hired Denise. Had they employed Joe, he would have likely failed in the position.

IQ Assessments:

Interestingly, research tells us that for jobs that are not routine, such as engineering and sales, cognitive capability is the single most significant predictor of success. Curiously, very few organizations use cognitive capability to measure the future likelihood of success. In an organization with whom I worked, we conducted a study that examined the correlation between cognitive capability and internal performance ratings. Through the research, we found a correlation of .32, a relatively high number that described the relationship between performance and IQ. Most interestingly, we found that the higher the IQ, the more the person had advanced in the organization, with some of the most intelligent people at the top of the pyramid.

Speciality Assessments:

There are numerous assessments that one can use to measure potential success. These assessments measure such items as sales capability, dexterity, math skills, and spreadsheet knowledge, to name a few. If you can describe the job, you can probably identify an assessment that will predict success, or at least a basic level of knowledge.

Personality Assessments:

Multiple instruments exist that measure personality traits. One of my favorite assessments is the Profile XT. (One of the nation's experts in the use of the ProfileXT is F. Bryan Summers. He can be reached at www.carolinaprofiles.com, or emailed at info@carolinaprofies.com. Bryan can help organizations with the details needed to effectively use the instrument.) The Profile XT enables the user to create both a personality and cognitive benchmark to which to compare candidates. Technicians create the baseline based on a combination of standard job descriptions from the U.S. Deparatment of Labor ONET online (www.onetonline.org,) and the results of a questionnaire given to the hiring organization. An easy-to-understand graphical report shows how close the candidate fits with job characteristics.

Interviewing

For most managers, interviewing is one of the most challenging aspects of hiring, often because they do it so infrequently. Each interview should be structured; that is, interviewers asked the same questions of each candidate. The questions relate directly to the job description described above so that hiring managers may ascertain whether this person fits within the minimum competency level.

Behavioral event interviewing is one of the most accessible and most popular methodologies. Each question relates to the essential elements of the job description, asking candidates to describe a time when they demonstrated that element. Not every item on the job description will have a corresponding question, just the most critical aspects.

Let's use the example job description example from table 1. We can also assume that we have already determined whether the individual completed a degree in accounting and has the appropriate experience level. For the knowledge and skills section, we may want to use an assessment to understand whether or not the person knows Excel basics. Let's attend to cultural fit, which is one of the most critical elements to assure success in an organization. Since the competency centers on teamwork and assertiveness, we may wish to ask questions such as the following:

Tell me about a time you worked in a team to achieve results. What were the results, and how did you engage with others?

> We would listen for the ability to collaborate, share responsibility, and assert oneself when one's ideas need to be heard. We can rate these answers on a scale of 1 to 5, with 5 representing the highest level of teamwork. 1 = did not demonstrate teamwork, 2 = demonstrated some teamwork, 3 = demonstrated average teamwork, 4 = demonstrated above-average teamwork, 5 = demonstrated superior teamwork.

Another question we might ask is: Tell me about a time when you worked in a team, and you thought others did not consider your opinion. What did you do?

> We might look for an answer that shows the candidates assert themselves and speak on behalf of their ideas even though others disagree. We do not want candidates to create destructive conflict, but we do want them forcefully to present their ideas for consideration.
>
> Again we can rate the answer on a scale of 1 to 5.

When hiring, having a team interview the candidate increases the likelihood of overall success. Before the interviews, the hiring team will want to define what the rating scale means for each of the questions. In the example above, an interview rating of 3, which is in the middle of the ratings, may mean different constructs among the interviewers. Having a clear understanding creates better interview results.

Averaging the scores for each question allows us to reduce the chances of rater bias. Rater bias often occurs when "gut feeling" biases results. The rater is inclined to view the candidate's answers as supporting the "gut feeling" and tends to rate the candidate higher than is appropriate.

Once the team calculates the averages, they meet to further discuss each candidate's fit with the organization. For example, if on the question above, three raters scored 3, 3, and 4, we assume we have consensus. On the other hand, if the evaluators scored the candidate 2, 4, and 5, the team would benefit from discussion to discover the reason for the variance. Perhaps one of the interviewers found an issue that the others did not.

Deliberate Practice for Expert Performance:

> As a high-performance leader, you will want to be an All-Star at hiring for your team. Of all the skills in leadership, this capability stands high on the list. Without the necessary foundations of top people, no leader can fully succeed.
>
> Here are a few exercises you may want to undertake:
>
> 1. Using one of your open positions as an example, create a detailed job description as described earlier in this chapter.
> 2. Using your job description, create behavioral-based questions for the most critical characteristics. Decide on a rating scale (typical rating is 1 to 5).
> 3. Practice working in a team to interview a job candidate.

Are you ready to hire the best? Assess yourself and understand your growth opportunities at www.expertperformance.com/hire-the-best.

CHAPTER 3

TRAIN FOR SUCCESS

Elevate your employees to produce top-notch performance

How often have you observed the following?

The XYZ company often hires recent college graduates. All candidates have a degree in engineering and have attained a level of technical competence, but they are not ready to function on their own. They require significant amounts of development. Look at an example.

Ashley joined the XYZ company two years ago, freshly out of engineering school. She had better-than-average grades, a cheerful and outgoing personality, and an ability to work with others. Even with this marvelous background, she still needed to understand the nuances of the XYZ engineering company. XYZ company people pride themselves on their high levels of customer service. They believe that any customer who called and asked for information that should have been given to them shows that XYZ company people have failed to anticipate their client's needs. Ashley had a great mentor in Megan and worked in partnership to help Ashley learn how to deal effectively with clientele. Ashley felt as though she could always pop into Megan's office and discuss her thinking regarding how the project should take shape. She became fully engaged in the XYZ company, and her future looked bright.

Though he had the same background as Ashley, Ryan had a much different experience in his attempts to reach full competency level. Ryan worked for Nicholas, who was in high demand by his clients and was rarely in the office. Ryan's opportunities to partner with Nicholas were spotty, and when he did have time to work with Nicholas, Ryan felt rushed. As a result, Ryan fell behind his contemporary, Ashley, and became frustrated by the lack of growth in training. He eventually quit the company.

As an organization, and as a leader, we feel fortunate when we hire top people to join our company. To have the new promising employees fully contribute takes considerably more effort than most leaders anticipate. As a colleague of mine says, no one is ready for prime time, not at least on day one.

In the example above, we read of something familiar, an employee joins an organization and is left to his own means to succeed – or, so often, fail and depart the organization. Many of those who could help an individual become competent to do the job find themselves already burdened by full workloads, leaving insufficient time to coach and develop. What do we do instead?

Let's return to the example job description from the previous chapter. Our new person has to learn how to lead a month-end closing and to produce job-costing reports for his or her assigned team. Interestingly, we anticipate that the employees (mentors/coaches) who will teach the new person will realize a direct hit to their productivity. Training a new person takes time, effort, and distracts mentors/coaches from their primary work. In the case of this hire, training will require 1/3 of the mentor/coach's time to bring the person up to full capability. In many organizations, the mentors/coaches will not be all to allowed to let this productivity decrease and will be expected to make up the time during off-hours. If mentor/coaches do not compensate for lost time, the organization will find its bottom-line suffering. On the other hand, working extra hours to make up a productivity deficit can cause burnout and dissatisfaction. Neither of these alternatives proves acceptable.

Instead, an organization will need to calculate the development burden for any new hire and then budget that cost. Let's take a look at the example from the previous chapter. Elevating the new person to conduct the month-end closing and produce job-cost reports results in a $20,000 expense to the company due to lost productivity. Other productivity impacts on teams in which the new person works will result in an additional $10,000 cost. Teaching practices of the department incur a $6000 productivity cost. Total costs are $36,000. Where is this cost charged? Unless there is a hard cost, such as training courses, most organizations do not include these onboarding costs in their budget. Once we calculate these real costs, we gain a better understanding of actual expenses as well as avoid the negative impact of overwork on our mentors/coaches.

There are several ways that individuals can become competent. Some are obvious and used universally, and others remain a bit more obscure.

Education

During my early days at IBM, I was required to attend several extensive training courses. My first course included several weeks of online programs followed by a month (yes, a month away from home) for classroom work. The entire process to bring someone to full competency for a systems engineer or marketing representative took approximately one year. Live classroom education, coupled with hands-on learning in branch offices, completed the year's effort. Today that training would cost about $200,000, which includes lost productivity, travel, and other associated costs.

My experience parallels those entering the trades such as plumbers, electricians, and HVAC technicians. However, there is one significantly different. Besides classes, most of these individuals apprentice to a journeyman in their trade, which brings us to apprenticeship.

Apprenticeship

One of my customers discovered a great way to bring people on board. After individuals enter the organization, the company assigns them to a more senior individual who guides the new employees through the transition from college to a professional career. First, the senior person assigns small aspects of current projects on which he or she is working. The new person performs the work, brings back the results of their assignment, and the two of them discuss suggestions on how to improve the next time. The new person accompanies the senior person on client calls, learning how to interact with customers.

This firm emphasizes client focus, followed by strict financial controls, and wraps it all together by hiring and creating high performance among their employees. The senior person helps the new individual understand how client service, tight financial controls, and their personal growth interact to create a top-performing organization.

To make an apprenticeship function correctly, you will want to do the following:

- Help the new person understand the values, mission, and vision of your organization, specifically how these interact to create top performance.

- Using the job description, document the competencies the person needs to achieve to become fully capable. For example, early on the new individual may need to understand how a project functions. They may learn how to account for and record the time they spend on the job, whether for customers or other activities. As the individual becomes more capable, the senior person may take the individual to the field to understand how projects function outside the office.

- In a stepwise manner, assign activities and tasks that raise the competencies to the appropriate levels needed for full function on the job. You will cover each competency in training. For example, we may wish the individual to learn how to talk to customers, and we might assign a task that the new person accompanies the senior person on a customer visit. After the visit, the two individuals would discuss the highpoints of the visit, pointing out essential learnings.

Coaching

I became a coach, mainly because several of my clients asked me if I could work with one of their employees. Usually, the scenario went something like this: Bob is having communications difficulties with other people; he tends to be short and offends those around him.

Often the issues were related to a challenge that the individual exhibited, which led me immediately into a trap called deficit coaching, which resulted in early failures. I remember a client who I was challenged to help who had communications problems. I sat across from the individual as we discussed the issues his management team identified. As I listed each of the issues, I could see the person in front of me change physically. First, he deflated, then he stiffened, then began to argue with me about each of the problems that I presented. The long list of issues, as well as expected changes from his boss, felt daunting. As a result, I was not successful, and neither was the company, and the individual left the organization. I quickly learned that deficit coaching does not work. No one wants to be fixed. My repair methodology did not work.

I later connected with a brilliant coach named Ann Clancy, who wrote a book with her co-authors called *Appreciative Coaching*. Through her mentoring, I discovered that none of us are broken or in need of repair. Through our work, I learned how to focus on my client's positive future.

Changing the emphasis to an optimistic approach brought the people with whom I work much more success.

Here are two scenarios – the wrong and the right way.

Deficit Coaching Conversation (How Not to Do Coaching)

> Coach: Marie, I understand from your manager that you are having some challenges in communicating with your colleagues. I know that they comment that you are sometimes short with them.
>
> Marie: I want to get things done, and sometimes my colleagues ask the same questions over and over again.
>
> Coach: Marie, perhaps we can fix this problem by helping you learn listening techniques.
>
> Marie: I think I'm a pretty good listener already. I'm not sure that you could teach me anything that I don't already have a handle on.
>
> Coach: Well, you may not have learned these listening techniques that I offer.
>
> Marie: I've been through about three or four listening classes.
>
> Coach: I think you will find my approach different than others.
>
> Marie: Everyone says I'm a good listener. I don't think you're listening to me.

By now, I think you understand that the conversation is going badly, and Marie is becoming more and more resistant. I realized that deficit coaching tends to cause people to be on guard and on edge. By using an appreciative approach, I was able to overcome resistance and use it to help my clients.

Appreciative Coaching

> Coach: Marie, I understand that you have great strengths, and your boss would like you to be even stronger than you are today.

Marie: Yes, I think I do a pretty good job, although sometimes I think I irritate people.

Coach: Help me understand how you think you sometimes irritate people.

Marie: I want to get things done, and sometimes people ask the same questions over and over again.

Coach: I'm sure that it can be annoying to you. Does it slow you down?

Marie: You are exactly on target. I want to get my work done, and these repetitive questions distract me.

Coach: You have some terrific strengths helping you to perform at a high level. Wouldn't it be great if everyone performed at that level?

Marie: It sure would. But how do I get those around me to pay more attention and work faster?

As you can see from the above, Marie has now entered into a problem-solving mode, which is much less emotional than one accentuating her deficits. Using the tools of influence, Marie can now elevate the performance of those around her. We'll discuss influence in a later chapter.

From our experience, very few managers seem to have the innate skills to coach, but with some training, most leaders can develop these capabilities. In a coaching session, here's what you want to do:

- Listen to understand the individual's perspective.
- Frame the person's challenges as strengths.
- Help the individual to use the strengths at an appropriate level. Overusing a strength can lead to irritation, such as that which Marie experienced. She wanted to produce but felt hindered by those around her.
- Help people to add to their influence toolbox.

Training and Education

I worked with an organization that began to struggle with disappointing sales results. The managers assumed that the issue centered on a lack of training. However, the organization had offered its sales group comprehensive and extensive education. Although the organization did a beautiful job of this, the training itself did not maximize expertise and high performance. In other words, it missed the mark, unable to help the salespeople become experts. In this case, the organization failed to focus on the most important learnings. We have found that, through Expert Performance Success Maps™, we can uncover the 20% that produces 80% of the results. If we teach this 20%, we spend less effort while we dramatically increase high performance.

In later chapters, we'll discuss how to reveal expertise, specifically how to uncover it and how to turn it into training and development.

Assuring Success

Today, most organizations offer development in the form of training and education, yet few offer apprenticeship and mentoring. Even when companies offer development, most organizations fail to assure the success of each new hire. My colleague was talking to a person who runs an organization that provides training, but if their people don't get it, then succeed, she quickly removes them. This example illustrates two fallacies. First, somehow the individual new hires became entirely responsible for assuring their personal success. Indeed, they share responsibility, but that sharing is with the leadership. After spending considerable resources to hire new employees, the manager left the success of the individual up to chance. Second, every leader becomes responsible for producing organizational outcomes through their people. By failing to interject themselves into the training and development process, the manager jeopardizes or, at the least, diminishes corporate results.

Here is what we recommend:

- Thoroughly understand the capabilities each person needs to achieve desired organizational outcomes.

- Provide training, education, and apprenticeship-like experiences that assure that the employees can become fully competent in their jobs.

- Insert frequent check-ins to assure that the person is learning and becoming more competent.

- Intervene when necessary, preferably early and more often than one would think appropriate.

The Cost of Creating Competency

In the previous chapter, we provided an example of the costs associated with bringing the individual up to full competency level. Unfortunately, few organizations capture and account for the investment required to bring an employee up to this full competency level. Instead, the organization buries expenses in different lines of the profit and loss statement. Sometimes, as we have seen with our clients, individuals who are responsible for the development of new hires spend extra effort to compensate for the time spent training a new person. As I mentioned in a previous example, one of our client's utilization rate dropped from 70% to 50% while preparing new employees. He will be forced to put in additional hours to keep his department at required budget levels. This company makes little or no effort to understand the total cost of growing someone to competency level.

Here is what we suggest:

- Fully uncover the real costs of bringing an individual to competency level.

- Allocate the cost, including recruitment costs, of bringing the individual to full competency level in the department in which the individual resides.

- Assure that your organization has sufficient resources in the department to add employees.

- Decide how to compensate for the reduced effectiveness of those doing the education and training. For example, if the cost, as in the previous chapter, were $37,000, as in the last case, the department must produce enough additional profit to offset the $37,000 of expense. Sometimes, this offset can be created by helping new employees to become profitable relatively quickly. Nevertheless, the organization must calculate how it will maintain performance.

Deliberate Practice for Expert Performance

In this chapter, I covered the necessity to understand the education, training, and coaching required to grow a person from new hire to become a competent and contributing employee. Most impressive, organizations find that employing apprenticeship approaches produce the fastest and most comprehensive results. By thoroughly understanding competency requirements for each hire, we can assure the individual success and the achievement of organizational outcomes.

As we have stated, bringing someone to competency level incurs real expense dollars. Most organizations spread the cost of new hire development across the entire company, failing to track the actual expenditures while lowering the overall effectiveness of the department in which the training occurs. Instead, we recommend that the organization account for these expenses in the department in which the spending occurs.

Here are a few practice activities I recommend:

1. Choose a job category. Identify the necessary steps to have an individual become competent in that job, including education, training, and on the job experience.

2. Calculate real expenses of bringing someone up to full capability. Costs should include lost opportunity, training and education, and value of the time spent by more senior personnel as they apprentice the novice employee.

3. Identify those who can mentor or coach a new employee, providing the mentor/coach with a well-defined roadmap for employee development.

4. Track the development of your new employees to assure that they are growing in their careers. (Having someone in charge of the development process dramatically enhances the opportunities for success.)

Are you ready to train your people for success? Assess yourself and understand your growth opportunities at

www.expertperformance.com/train-for-success.

CHAPTER 4

ENGAGE AND GROW YOUR EMPLOYEES

Become THE company where everyone wants to work

Ever wonder why you lose people in your organization or why your relationships with customers are not as good as you would like? Do you think about why your profit is not as high as it could be? Even if you have the performance you want, you will still want to find easy ways to grow your business beyond its current size. In recent years, the concept of engagement has come to the forefront of leadership thinking. Thanks to organizations such as the Gallup company and others, we can understand who is engaged in your organization and who is not.

For our purposes, engagement is the willingness of your employees to bring discretionary effort into your company. Here are several examples of different engagement levels. Which of these associates do you want on YOUR team?

Amanda joined the organization five years ago. She usually arrives early at work so that she can prepare herself for the day. She will work extra hours when needed to make sure that she and her team are successful. She engages with her teammates frequently, asking if there's something extra she can do to help the group to move forward. Customers often call her when they need advice. Her boss says she has a loyal following. Headhunters regularly call her, but she politely responds that she's not interested. Over the years, Amanda has offered numerous suggestions to improve her company's growth, ideas that have often been adopted. She feels well trained and that her career is moving along nicely. She buys into the mission of the company, believing that it dovetails nicely with her personal vision. Amanda is not looking for another position, nor would she likely take one if offered. She likes the people at her current organization and feels like she's making a difference.

Daniel joined his organization about five years ago. He faithfully arrives at work on time and just as faithfully leaves precisely at the end of the day. He's had a few calls from headhunters and has responded with interest, although nothing has panned out yet. He feels like he's not contributing as much as he could to the organization, nor is the organization training him as much as he would like. Sometimes he wonders what his organization stands for beyond making money for the owners. Daniel never fails to respond positively when asked to do extra tasks, but he never volunteers for additional work. If asked to help, he helps. If a new position came along at a company he admired, he would not hesitate to leave.

Bill can't wait to find a new job and tells everyone he knows that he is actively looking for a new position. At lunch, he lets his colleagues know what a horrible company they all work in. He never volunteers for extra work, and when he is assigned a new task, will grumble to everyone. He barely comes in on time, cleans off his desk ten minutes before quitting time, then bounds out the door exactly at 5:00.

Using an analogy, a representative from the Gallup organization explained that there are three classes of engagement: engaged, unengaged, and disengaged. Engaged employees are like homeowners, homeowners who paint, cut the grass, pick up trash, and take full responsibility for their dwelling. Engaged employees feel responsibility for their team and company. Unengaged employees fall in the same family as renters. They pay their rent but don't go the extra lengths to take care of the place in which they live. Like renters, unengaged employees perform reasonably well while they are present, but they don't take on the obligation for their team or their company's outcomes. The final category, disengaged employees, are like squatters. They take up space and cause damage. You need to get them out because their bad attitude will poison others.

In the example above, Amanda represents a fully engaged employee willing to give discretionary effort to the organization. She feels personally connected both to the company's work and to her fellow team members. When she is needed, she volunteers to work beyond her usual assignments. She regularly thinks of ways to improve her efforts, her team, and her company. Ryan, on the other hand, is unengaged. He feels underused, untrained, and unappreciated. He's not a poor employee, just one who feels disconnected from the organization. Bill feels actively disengaged. He will actively lower the engagement of others.

Why Engagement

Why pay attention to engagement? According to the Gallup organization, a staggering 87% of employees worldwide are not engaged at work (Crabtree, 2013). Here is what Gallup found for those organizations having the highest engagement compared to those who have the lowest.

- They outperform counterparts by 187% in earnings per share.
- Highly engaged organizations have 48% fewer safety incidents.
- 41% fewer quality incidents
- Higher turnover organizations report 25% lower turnover.
- Lower turnover organizations report a stunning 65% lower turnover.
- 21% more profitability
- 20% more productivity
- 10% higher customer loyalty

Numerous organizations provide engagement offerings that will meet the needs of your organization. A recent experience with the AON corporation provided engagement scores as well as an environmental and organizational assessment. This assessment included an examination of such items as employee attitudes towards benefits, salary, work/life balance, and diversity. Gallup uses 12 simple questions used to predict the future performance of an organization, making the instrument quick and easy to administer.

To pick the best engagement assessment, you will want to understand the following:

- Does the tool compare your results with others? Some tools provide a percentile ranking that shows how your company stands compared to similar organizations. If, for example, your company scored at the 75th percentile ranking or above, your organization would be in the top 25%, the top quartile.

- Does the company providing the assessment give you direction on how to increase retention?

- Can you repeat the assessment multiple times without incurring additional costs?

- Does the engagement tool allow you to filter for different parts of the organization, such as allowing you to report how employees of each manager answered?

The table below illustrates several typical example questions and the company's scoring. Raw scores are often measured between one and five. Percentile rankings explain how your company compares to others. For example, referring to the first question below, the company scored better than 55% of all organizations and lower than 45% of all firms.

Question	Average	Percentile Rank
If my friend were looking for employment, I would recommend my company.	3.5	55%
The mission of my company motivates me to work harder.	2.5	40%
My company provides me with what I need to do my work well.	4.1	64%
I feel like my company uses my ideas.	3.9	59%
My company's benefits program meets my needs.	2.5	35%
(More Questions)		
Overall Scores	4.2	63%

Once your organization has completed the engagement survey, analyze results, noting areas of strength as well as challenges. From the table above, perhaps you notice that the answers to "the mission of my company motivates me to work harder" is one of the questions that has lowered the overall engagement scores.

You may wish to conduct focus groups with your associates so that you can understand the detail behind answers to engagement questions. Doing so provides you with clarity, a refined direction, and avoids assumptions that could lead to unnecessary costs or work. For example, one of our clients scored low on a question from the AON survey regarding satisfaction with benefits. (In the AON survey, the benefits question is part of a group of organizational conditions that, when positive, lead to employee satisfaction.) We had assumed that dissatisfaction with benefits meant health insurance, but to our surprise, employee focus group members cited paid time off as the main reason for the low scoring results. Conducting the focus group allowed us to avoid traveling down a road to repair health insurance that would have been costly and unnecessary.

Once you fully understand the engagement challenges, management can intervene to make a difference. Let me share an example.

Let's return to the example of Daniel above. Let's assume that the company in which he works decided to conduct an engagement survey which showed that most of the organization failed to understand the purpose of their work. In this example, assume that senior leadership agreed to simplify the mission statement, reducing several paragraphs to an easy to remember phrase: "We save the environment for future generations." This shortened phrase was designed to help employees easily grasp the meaning of the company mission and to build a personal connection between each employee and the work of their organization. Multiple focus groups throughout the company showed majority support for the shortened mission statement. Had the leadership ended their effort at this point, they would have missed an essential element of the connection of the mission to the employees: the need for continuous reinforcement. As part of a concerted effort to help everyone embrace the importance of the company's work, the leadership began a comprehensive program to emphasize how the company saved the environment. For example, each employee meeting, no matter how brief, started with the mission of the company followed by participant descriptions of ways they have fulfilled their mission.

During one meeting, Daniel discussed an innovative and ecologically friendly design for a wastewater treatment tank. Even though his part of the project was relatively small, his presentation allowed him to start to understand how his efforts in processing contaminated liquid made the environment safer. He began to realize that his labors, no matter how small, really were saving the environment. As Daniel gained broader knowledge and experience, he would add more stories, and his personal engagement and morale would continue to grow.

How to Grow Engagement and Produce More Profit

When I worked at an electrical contractor, we conducted an engagement survey which showed our organization stood slightly below the middle of the pack, a position that seemed unsatisfactory. To raise engagement, we began two intensive activities.

We required that individuals receive 360 feedback measuring how they stacked up against a benchmark of the best employees. We produced an expert performance map that defined how the best employees performed. The map became the basis of the benchmark. 360 feedback means that multiple individuals rate the employee. Usually, these raters include self, manager, direct reports, peers, and others. Occasionally, 360 feedback includes customer responses. (Later in this book, I will explain the basics necessary to create an Expert Performance Success Map™.) During feedback sessions with their managers, employees discussed their strengths as well as challenges, paying particular attention to any issues which stood in the way of their career progression. Once we identified these issues, we created development plans to grow the individual's career possibilities. For example, many newer project managers had not had the opportunity to perform cost estimates, which were usually completed by more senior leaders or by a specialized group of estimators. To overcome this learning deficit, senior leaders gave their more junior counterparts assignments to estimate a change order. A change order is, as the name suggests, a change to the current project plan that usually requires additional funding. It is generally small in scope, allowing the junior project manager a chance to learn a new skill without having a significant negative impact should they make a mistake.

Concurrently with the above actions, we formed teams of our organization's high potentials to address company issues that were important but not urgent. For example, a high-potential team might find ways to improve the organization's brand, allowing us to attract better job candidates.

As a result of our efforts, an engagement survey conducted eighteen months later showed a 10-percentage point rise.

Here are a few essential steps to growing engagement that we have found in our research and experiences:

- **Assure that your organization's mission and vision are apparent, easily remembered, and compelling.** Here are a few such easy-to-grasp statements: "We're changing the way America leads." "We raise everyone's capabilities to the highest levels." "We save lives." "We're saving the environment." Long-winded narratives that fail to inspire, at best, end up on your wall gathering dust, and, at the worst, cause your people to pull back and disengage from your company. Senior leadership's continuing communication of the inspirational mission and vision gives the words life, relevance, and meaning across your company.

Specifying a mission for an organization provides a clear and consistent roadmap for individuals in the organization. It allows employees to feel that their work is essential and that they are making a difference. During consulting engagements, I often ask employees to tell me the mission of their organization. What do you think your organization is trying to accomplish, and why is it in business? In a recent conversation with employees, I asked a disheartened group the purpose of their work. This organization has a solid core of service that works to make our environment safe for future generations. The group answered that they believed the purpose of the organization was to make money for the owners. When I hear an answer like this, I realize that the company has failed to post a compelling mission and vision and has not spent sufficient time to enable employees to understand the meaningfulness of the work they perform.

- **Make development planning for your employees an inseparable part of your culture.** After all, you can trace every figure on your profit and loss statement to human activity. The better the employees perform, the better your P&L will be.

  I recommend setting a development plan in place for each person. In the electrical contractor organization, we defined the competency and learning path a project manager would need to follow to move from an assistant project manager to project manager, to senior project manager, and finally to a VP in the organization. Within six months of joining the company, project managers knew where they stood on the path and had written goals to move up the path, presenting them with a well-defined opportunity to excel in their career.

  When creating a development plan, bear in mind that some individuals have the temperament for senior leadership and others do not. One of the individuals with whom we worked was a bit testy and had difficulty working with others. When placed on a single person project that was facing challenges, he performed well. He was an asset to the organization. When placed on a team, he often created tension. We understood that his presence on these small challenging projects made him a valuable asset, but he would not lead a group until he developed additional people skills. Until such time, he would remain an individual contributor.

- **Set clear expectations for performance.** We all wish to contribute. Knowing when we have reached performance expectations makes us all feel good about ourselves and our company. Perhaps even more important is the need to know our decision-making boundaries. One of my colleagues told me of an experienced and highly accomplished individual hired as a sales VP for a small business. His considerable industry and management experience made him a likely high-valued addition to the firm. Assuming the newly created role of sales VP, he began his new company tenure by moving bolding to add revenue and profit to his new company. In a particularly competitive situation, and after much thought, the new VP discounted his product so he could bring on board a new customer, a customer who had a high future revenue and profit potential. He felt quite proud of his team's accomplishment, but unfortunately, the owner did not share his opinion. Instead, he reprimanded the new VP. "You do not discount any of our products without a discussion with me. Pricing goes through me".

  How demoralizing this experience must have been. The new VP found his decision-making "sandbox" to be much smaller than he initially assumed and realized that his every choice would be scrutinized and second-guessed. As you can imagine, the VP would not have taken the position had he known about the owner's close management style. Had the owner told the VP upfront about his decision-making boundaries, they could have avoided a difficult situation. The VP ultimately left.

- **Hire and develop great leaders who care about and listen to their people.**

  In a seminal research article, Herzberg found that one of the strongest demotivators for those at work was poor experiences with one's supervisor (Herzberg, 2002). A supporting article by the Gallup organization points out that 70% of the variance in engagement scores is because of one's manager (Beck, 2015). That is a correlation of nearly .84 (1 is the highest). Leaders can make an astounding difference.

  One of our customers has two senior leaders who are excellent examples of top managers. A younger member of the team, who joined the organization about four years ago, talks of the ease with which he can approach these two leaders for help and advice. When he joined the organization, the leaders gave him small projects on which to work. As he progressed through each effort, the leaders would provide guidance on best practices. He stated that at no time did the leaders make him feel as though his questions were a burden or that his mistakes were anything more than a need for a course correction. As he progressed, his leadership gave him increasingly more complex projects, continuing to guide and correct in ways that caused him to feel committed entirely and absorbed. As a result, he quickly became capable and competent as well as highly engaged with his team and his company.

Here is what we found that contributes to expert leadership:

- Leaders challenge their employees, expecting results that push them to the edge of their capabilities.

- No leader lets his employees fail, even while pushing for high performance.

- Top leaders assure their employees that they will succeed and are always present to help.

- Top leaders listen carefully to gain understanding and create an atmosphere in which the employee can be vulnerable. This atmosphere encourages employees to admit mistakes readily, which allows for a quick resolution.

- Top leaders raise the bar after each project, increasing the employee's capabilities and competencies.

- Top leaders are readily available to their employee to listen to concerns and provide advice and clarity.

- Top leaders genuinely care about and are concerned for their employees. They demonstrate this caring by assuring that the employee succeeds and grows in their career.

- Top leaders express employee appreciation every day.

Recognize and Praise your people

Herzberg also discovered that one of the top positive employee experiences relates to reward and recognition. Reward and recognition go a long way towards creating more engagement and ultimately improving profit for your company.

When I worked for IBM, IBM worked hard to encourage and reward individuals in their organization. Most of these awards included public recognition and financial benefits. However, sometimes the best recognition comes in unexpected ways. Sometimes small gestures can make a more significant difference than one would ordinarily expect. A telephone call, a hand-written note, or an appreciative email can dramatically improve an employee's outlook. I remember a report I sent to my second-level manager. Even though I don't recall the content of the report, I do remember this. On an attached sticky note, and in the boss's handwriting, were two words: "good job." No one in IBM had sent me such a note before. Decades later, I still remember this recognition much more than any of the financial and formal awards.

Here are a few questions to ask yourself:

- Do you have a formal employee recognition program?
- Do you express your appreciation to each of your reports at least once a week?
- Do you thank people for doing their job?
- Do you respond with a written thank you when an employee delivers a work product?
- Do you talk to your people at least every six months about their future and how you will help them reach their vision?

Deliberate Practice for Expert Performance:

You may want to conduct the following to develop your business.

- Consider conducting an engagement survey so that you may understand the discretionary effort currently expended by your people. Follow the engagement survey with focus groups to hone in on the underlying reasons for the engagement scores.

- Make your vision and mission statements compelling and easily remembered by all of your employees. Consistently and regularly communicate the mission and vision to your people in ways that allow them to understand the connection between these statements and the employees' work.

- Assure that you have development plans for every employee.

- Make sure that expectations for performance are well defined. Pay particular attention to decision-making boundaries.

- Hire top leaders who care about and listen to their employees.

- Review the section on what we have found in our research that contributes to expert leadership.

- Assure that you have formal and informal recognition programs.

Are you ready to train engage and grow your people? Assess yourself and understand your growth opportunities at

www.expertperformance.com/engage-and-grow.

CHAPTER 5

THE POWER OF STRENGTHS

Focus on what you and your people are profoundly good at and achieve superior outcomes

Eric exhibited marvelous beginnings as his talent became more apparent in his later college years. He had a unique ability to understand the big picture in any electrical engineering issue, often making insightful and strategic decisions that others found remarkable. In his classroom work, his teammates often stood back while Eric took on the assigned project's heavy lifting. When team members tried to contribute, Eric would quickly explain the reasons why his approach was superior. Ultimately, his cohorts would learn that feedback to Eric fell on deaf ears, as they realized that Eric would always arrive at a solution that was far superior to any ideas the group had.

Given his considerable capabilities, companies widely recruited Eric for internships, which usually turned into significant job offers. One of the interested companies, DRC Engineering, offered Eric a dream position. The compensation, work environment, and reputation fulfilled Eric's concept of an ideal organization. During the final interview, Terry, the owner, sat across from Eric, telling him of the full range of opportunities that awaited him at DRC Engineering, including opportunities to advance into higher levels of management. Eric spent little time thinking over the offer from DRC Engineering and excitedly told Terry that he would gladly accept.

Customers recognized DRC Engineering as a leader whose specialized efforts lowered energy consumption across wide ranges of industries, reducing power needs and ultimately supporting environmental initiatives. Eric found a strong connection to DRC Engineering and looked forward to the opportunity to use his vast talents as well as make a substantial difference for future generations.

Working under the leadership of an experienced engineering executive (and company owner), Eric flourished, living up to his promise to deliver top-quality projects. Eric loved the fast-paced problem-solving that challenged and expanded his thinking each day. As their first significant project date approached, the team rallied to produce an on-time effort that exceeded public and investor expectations. Eric and DRC Engineering's future looked bright, and after two years, Terry asked Eric to join him in conversation in one of the company's quiet rooms.

Terry began, "Eric, I love your strategic thinking since it creates significant positive results for clients, but it also positions us for continued future business." Eric felt a bit uneasy with praise, then responded with a quiet, "Thank you." Terry continued, "You probably have realized that we need to grow our company, and I can't take on additional reports. Since you have performed so well, I would like to offer you a team lead position. You will be responsible for taking on a group, expanding it, and working with a long-term valued customer. Are you interested?"

Eric felt excited and hopeful. Eric's father had been an executive in a large company, and Eric always wanted to follow in his dad's footsteps. A move to team lead would be the first step to achieving that dream. Unfortunately, this was the beginning of trouble for Eric.

The new group formed readily, with the more seasoned associates running as quickly as they always had, but new associates struggled with DRC Engineering's fast-paced projects. Many were dazzled by Eric's incredible capabilities, yet felt demoralized as they tried to keep up.

As success grew, pressure from a long-term client pushed Terry to address Eric's shortcomings. "After talking with a few of your team members, I decided you need to hear feedback. As a long-term customer, XYZ looks to us to expand their strategic thinking, adding more and more value to their business. Our XYZ contact confided that, even though your team delivers best-in-class results, XYZ feels as though they are not receiving the payoff from us they have come to expect. Because you take on many of the tasks, your team has fallen behind on a few of the basic activities. It's time to transfer that wonderful expertise you have to everyone in your group. All of the associates recognize how good you are at what you do, yet they tell me that when they ask you to explain how they can get the same results, you tell them what to do rather than teach them to perform more effectively. I know you all feel frustrated. Your group isn't getting better, and I had hoped you would help them grow. We have to correct this issue." Terry paused a moment waiting for Eric's reply.

"I agree that our team has not been performing as well as we would like." He corrected himself, "As well as I would like. I've tried to teach others what I know, but they don't seem to get it. They don't think the way I do, and when I talk about my thinking, all I see are blank stares or puzzled looks. I'm not much of a teacher, I guess."

Terry responded, "Whatever you need to do, help your team speed up. We need this challenge turned around in the next month." Terry provided a few more encouraging words, yet left Eric thinking he was pretty much on his own to correct his challenges.

Shy when meeting people, Eric often needed time to warm up to others, and he frequently felt awkward in group settings, preferring one-on-one conversations. He had found an easy way out by telling his direct reports rather than engaging them in a learning conversation.

Eric walked out of the huddle room, thinking about what he might do differently, but nothing came to mind immediately.

The next month passed, but not much changed. Eric even accelerated his own furious pace, but he could not compensate for the slower progress of the newer associates. Two of them became frustrated and left DRC Engineering for another startup, and another began complaining to his friends about the lack of training at the company. Morale continued its downward path.

Terry felt even more pressure, and, once again, returned with Eric in the quiet room. "Eric, I know you have tried very hard to enhance your team, and we appreciate your effort. You are a valuable member of our organization. I'm sorry, but your efforts have not returned the team performance we need, and we would like you to work with an executive coach to help you increase your skills.

Eric felt a mixture of defeat and, simultaneously, a sense of hope. Perhaps someone could help him reach his goals.

I began discussions with Eric to understand his approach. His shyness, intelligence, and directness would often leave others puzzled and confused, not knowing how to interpret conversations with him. DRC

Engineering has a culture focused on apprenticeship, where the company walks associates through a step-by-step process to become proficient at their work. Eric's direct approach worked against the culture of the organization, leaving employees feeling undervalued and untrained. Because of Eric's personality, he would often shy away from teaching moments, failing to take the extra time to help the employee work through their struggles.

I suggested that Eric employ his considerable strengths, channeling his efforts through a collaborative team approach rather than a top-down teaching effort. This method enlisted the collective wisdom of the team to grow, develop and self-manage the entire group. The results were profound. An enthusiastic, involved team evolved, allowing Eric to focus his attention where his strengths lay, thinking strategically how the group might better serve the customer. By enlisting the entire team to solve customer relationship issues, the team exhibited new engagement and energy. Eric was well on the path to success.

So, what happened at DRC Engineering that caused Eric to be in such an awkward position? Let's first begin with Eric's strengths. Eric is an exceptional thinker with genius-like skills. His top strength is an ability to envision strategic challenges faced by his clients. On the other hand, as early as his college years, Eric showed that he does not have a strength to teach others how to achieve similar results, making it difficult to develop his colleagues. Every leader MUST grow his team. Unfortunately for Eric, he was placed in a position by Terry precisely to do just that, develop others on his group without having the capability to do so. He felt lost. No one in the small DRC Engineering knew how to grow Eric's self-understanding. His desire to become an executive compounded his challenges when he was offered an attractive promotion for which he wasn't ready.

In my experience, organizations, particularly smaller organizations, place people in positions to which they are ill-suited. Understanding one's strengths is crucial to creating a high-performance career, fostering an innate drive for excellence and top performance. One of the individuals who I interviewed talked about a situation in which he found himself. He had lost his head of sales and needed a replacement. The organization had a good salesperson, I'll call him Bill, who excelled at writing contracts and built excellent relationships with large customers. Unfortunately, he was unable to hold underlings accountable for their sales performance. A large company would replace the person or hire someone over him, but for small companies, swapping out talent is not practical. Doing so may cause a large amount of organizational memory to walk out the door.

Instead, Glenn recognized Bill's strengths and challenges, and as a result, Glenn promoted the individual. Instead of allowing Bill to try to hold his people accountable, Glenn put himself in place to hold the sales team responsible. With Glenn compensating for Bill's challenges and Bill working towards his strengths, Bill and the organization succeeded.

Several fundamental ways allow us to uncover our strengths and will enable us to identify our high performance.

Assessments: One of the easiest ways to uncover our strengths is through assessments. A quick Internet search provides multiple citations of tools to help gain more self-understanding. One of my favorites is the Strengthfinder 2.0 which, through a brief, inexpensive survey, identifies your top 5 strengths. (Visit https://store.gallup.com then order the Strengthsfinder 2.0 book which will have a code to take the assessment.) When taking the Strengthfinder as a group, the team can discover how its strengths fall into four categories: relationship, strategic, influence, and execution. With each category covered, the organization increases its likelihood of success.

Feedback: I am, as are most of us, ill-suited to understand my strengths fully, so receiving feedback provides an avenue for understanding. I once asked a customer why he liked working with me, and his response surprised me. First, he said, you bring a great deal of outside information and ideas that refresh our outlook. Second, you are candid and do not withhold valuable information for fear of hurting our feelings or relationship. Interestingly, these observations correspond with my results on the Strengthsfinder. One of my strengths is called Learner. I love to learn and share learnings with others. Bringing information to my clients has become second nature. The Gallup organization describes a second strength, Achiever, as a strong drive to achieve. Sometimes I want the client to grow more quickly than even they want, so I am candid and push to drive results.

Three types of under-optimized strengths

From my client work, I have discovered three ways strengths are not realized and maximized. These three areas are:

1. Hidden, also called underused, strengths.

2. Misplaced strengths, strengths that are used in one aspect of a person's life but not in another.

3. Finally, perhaps the most common, overused strengths.

Hidden Strengths

Don faced a watershed career moment, a moment that would make anyone except Don feel proud and happy. Instead, he was unsure whether he should take the new assignment. Don worked in a law firm, and the individual whose name was on the front door wanted to retire in a few years. To choose a new leader, the other partners took a poll, and Don's name came to the top of the list.

Throughout Don's early life, his parents taught him to be humble, to stay at the back of the line, reminding him that the "humble shall be exalted." During his career at the firm where he had spent most of his working life, every year brought increasing responsibility. He never asked for it; it just came.

Throughout high school, college, and work he had regularly been asked to take leadership roles, even though he never sought advancement. Now he faced a daunting responsibility helping to keep a firm growing at 20% per year as it had done under the owner's watchful eye. Self-doubt began to grow. Could he lead such an organization? Could he continue it down this path of success?

To everyone around him, Don had tremendous leadership capabilities, but he failed to embrace and relish this critical strength. His humbleness stood in his way.

During my days in IBM, I once asked a very successful sales representative how he could bring in and close so many opportunities. I expected a detailed "how-to" list that would help me achieve similar results. Instead, this humble man replied, "I just talked to people."

Humbleness is a great attribute, but when it keeps us from maximizing and using strengths, we can't offer ourselves entirely, achieve personal growth, nor can our organizations benefit to the maximum extent. Don and I worked together to help him fully acknowledge his unique leadership strengths, to embrace them, and use them to advance the organization.

Today, the firm continues its stellar growth, thanks to Don's continuing leadership.

During a conversation with a retired Army colonel, we discussed this very issue. Hidden strengths often impact women more than men. Many women with whom I've talked believe that doing good work will be discovered and appreciated by senior officials. Instead, when leadership is predominantly male, these capable women often are overlooked.

Once you have discovered your strengths, maximize them, and let others know how to use these strengths to help them succeed.

Misplaced Strengths

I often work with people who have experienced athletic or other careers, such as music, that require tremendous discipline and focused practice. These individuals have developed a laser-like mindset that allowed them to set aside other distractions and hone in on their music or athletic efforts. Interestingly, I find these individuals frequently fail to use the strengths and capabilities at work, strengths that made them so accomplished in their other endeavors.

We call these strengths -

> Misplaced strengths, i.e., the strengths are available in one aspect of their lives (such as in athletics or music) but are unavailable in other areas such as their job.

Sometimes we think an attractive path will open to us, but our strengths do not support what we need to do to achieve.

When I was in graduate school, I studied opera with one of the premier teachers in the country. Even today, many years later, his students can be found in premier opera houses across the globe. Just the other day, I was listening to a re-broadcast from the Lyric Opera of Chicago and heard one of his students singing the role of Rigoletto. Because one has the talent and the teacher does not translate into automatic success, I did not have the discipline to take those steps necessary to develop a viable and robust career in the world of opera. I had the voice but not the drive.

But I had other strengths.

Years later I worked with a coach, Ann Clancy, (I highly recommend her book called *Appreciative Coaching*) who developed, together with two colleagues, the concept of appreciative coaching. One of the tenants of appreciative coaching posits that no one is broken or needs repair. We all have strengths that, although sometimes misplaced, can make us exceptional. In our work together, Ann helped me discover significant strengths that I used in one aspect of my life but not in another.

I was always good at thinking about my future, which the Gallup organization calls Futuristic strength, yet was not applying this strength to my coaching. According to Gallup, "People who are especially talented in the Futuristic theme are inspired by the future and what could be. They inspire others with their visions of the future."

My second strength is Maximizer. Gallup defines Maximizer as, "People who are especially talented in the Maximizer theme focus on strengths as a way to stimulate personal and group excellence. They seek to transform something strong into something superb."

I became more aware of these essential strengths, and I began to use them in my coaching practice. I found that most people underestimate their strengths or have them misplaced in some other aspects of their lives. This misplacement makes their lives less fulfilling and satisfying. Helping them maximize the strengths and use them in all aspects of their lives can be a profound personal experience and can change their future.

One of my colleagues, who runs an organization and is required to speak often, has an incredible mind and can work harmoniously with highly educated scientists. When she did not know the audience, she told me that she felt as though she could not be a confident speaker. In other words, to be confident required her to know the audience ahead of time so that she could prepare a message directed at that audience's needs. Unfortunately, when asked to speak extemporaneously, she often did not know the audience ahead of time and could not prepare the way she usually did, which made her feel uncomfortable.

But here was the hidden strength. She has an incredible ability to prepare well, and in doing so, feels confident. This ability is a profound strength. We discovered a way to help her be prepared for any situation. She only needed three speeches, speeches that she could compose ahead of time allowing her to feel confident. All she had to do was ask a couple of open-ended questions at a meeting, and she could discover which speech she should use. Since she already practiced the speeches, she would remain fully engaged and confident.

As I suggested earlier, I highly recommend that you take the Strengthfinder's 2.0 assessment from the Gallup organization.

- Take a look at your top strengths and decide whether you may have compartmentalized these strengths into one part of your life and are not using them in another.

- Use these misplaced strengths to make a profound difference in you!

Overused Strengths

Mitchell knew something was wrong. He was concerned, and his future felt more uncertain than at any time in his career. What was he doing wrong? Nine months ago, Mitchell received a promotion after a highly successful project completion. He and his previous team had delivered outstanding results. Although he had a few of his talented staff leave for other opportunities, Mitchell had achieved his goals, and he felt terrific about that. Now he was managing other managers. To his dismay, his new group failed to reach its targets for the last two quarters, and the third quarter looked even worse.

Mitchell walked into his manager's office. Laura looked up and smiled warmly at Mitchell, and he returned the greeting halfheartedly. Mitchell felt on edge and wasn't sure how this conversation might turn. Laura began, "Mitchell, the reason I wanted to talk to you is that you are a very successful contributor to our organization. We want to build on that success." Mitchell relaxed a bit yet waited for the "but. "

Laura continued, "We've noticed that lately you and your team haven't performed up to your usual high marks. When I see this kind of performance, I am inclined to talk to people in your department to understand the reasons for the lower performance. In this case, I found something exciting, something that you can easily correct."

Mitchell breathed an internal sigh of relief and could feel himself relax a little. Perhaps the situation would turn out okay.

"Your previous team was composed of relatively new people. You intervened often, directing the team and helping them to succeed. You managed very closely because the team needed it. For some, this close management was helpful. Others decided to leave. Out of curiosity, why did you manage this previous team the way you did?"

Mitchell thought for a moment then responded, "I wanted to make sure that they achieved the outcomes needed. I knew that the team required direction since most were relatively inexperienced. I knew we needed to get things done!"

Laura said, "You are right on target. That group needed your close supervision. Providing close direction is one of your strengths. You know how to achieve results, and you can push others to do so. You know how to manage closely and give precise directions." She continued, "Sometimes strengths can be overused. Now that you have a group of highly skilled and experienced managers under you, they need less direct intervention. From interviewing your team, I found that they were reluctant to act unless they had your approval, causing them to wait for your responses before they could move forward. By managing so closely, you slowed down their processes, and that is why you have not reached your goals. At the same time, your team has become demoralized because they feel they haven't been able to achieve."

"You have overused a strength that is highly appropriate in one instance and yet not in another."

Mitchell responded, "I understand what you mean. Now that you pointed it out, I can recognize that I'm slowing folks down. What should I do instead?"

"You can dial back your close management style by providing enough clarity so that your team can reach their goals without needing your intervention. Intervene when they require help or are on the verge of failure, but not before."

"I get it," said Mitchell. "I've become a bottleneck to decision-making, and by providing more clarity, I can help the group feel more empowered, able to make their own decisions."

"Now you've got it. Let's spend a little more time to nail down some of the specifics on how to manage leaders. More importantly, you'll learn how to use a strength without overdoing it."

As illustrated in this story, many of us have incredible strengths, but, if overused, they can cause inadvertent harm. In the case of Mitchell, his overuse of a strength for achieving results through close management caused his team to fail.

What strengths do you overuse?

Deliberate Practice for Expert Performance

You may want to undertake the following to develop your strengths further.

- Consider an assessment of yourself that will identify your strengths. The Gallup organization provides a great resource. An author named Marcus Buckingham offers another terrific instrument, Standout 2.0 (https://www.tmbc.com/product/standout-2-0/), to uncover your strengths. You can get a code to take the assessment by purchasing his book, *Standout 2.0: Asssess Your Strengths, Find Your Edge Win at Work* (2015, Harvard Review Press). Marcus Buckingham, author of *First Break all the Rules* and *Now, Discover your Strengths*, offers an insightful look at strength-based approaches to performance appraisals, training programs and succession planning.

- Ask your colleagues, friends, family, and bosses what they notice are your strengths.

- Be sure to ask the same individuals whether you are underusing strengths, have misplaced some strengths, or are overusing some of your capabilities.

- Explore how you can shift to an accurate balance for you and your team. Don't be a fraid to ask how and to get support.

Are you ready to master the power of strengths? Assess yourself and understand your growth opportunities at

www.expertperformance.com/power-of-strengths.

CHAPTER 6

BE MORE PROFITABLE

Create a culture where your people will work twice as hard to produce profit

One of my clients, I'll call him Jim, runs a small division of his larger organization. Jim is a terrific guy who cares about each person who reports to him—the whole person, not just each person's work contributions. He has built a well-functioning team and a robust culture that fosters strong loyalty to him and the company. Recent engagement scores showed his group at the top of all divisions.

We know from our research, and from working with teams and organizations, that a robust engagement precedes strong financial performance. Unfortunately, Jim's group continued to produce less-than-desired profits, even though the results were respectable. At 10%, they were not meeting budget. Jim needed 15%. The team and my client desperately wanted to be at the top of monetary contributions to the company. I wanted them to succeed, too.

The client, the team, and I felt stymied. I am reminded of experiments conducted by Martin Seligman, a renowned psychologist who discovered a concept called learned helplessness (Seligman, 1979). In his experiments, dogs that had learned that they could not escape shock were placed into a position in which they *could* remove themselves from the painful experience. Even though the new situation allowed the dogs to move to a safer area, some dogs did not do so. From this observation, he coined this behavior as learned helplessness. Learned helplessness occurs in our business environment when people believe that no matter what they do, nothing will work. Jim's team had tried about everything they could think of, and nothing was effective. They began to blame the organization, even though the solution was within their grasp.

I consulted the CFO of the organization, explaining that we were at a loss to understand why the group could not reach their profit goals. He instructed his accounting group to provide the team with several simple, yet profoundly revealing, reports. (If you do not have these reports, you should. They are invaluable.) The first report showed the profitability of each of the client's customers ranked from top to bottom. See the sample report below. To their surprise, about a third of the clients were at or below the target profitability, with some showing a significant loss.

Having never seen the profit contributions of each customer, team members found this information shocking. During a meeting of the entire group, one of Jim's staff looked at the bottom third and called out, "Hey, those are my clients! If I try to raise prices on those individuals, I'll lose half of them." After much discussion, the team reached a general agreement that a few clients might have to depart.

Figure 1 Profitability Report

Duckling Imprints	20%
NoGo Taxi	18%
Make No Sense Analytics	17%
LZ E Service	17%
Poors Design	17%
Lobster Bisque Co	17%
Bobs Boxing Square	16%
Knotty Carpentry	15%
Flips 2 Day Plumbing Service	15%
XYZ Alphabet Lettering	15%
Long Time Waite Medical	13%
Madison Square Gardening	11%
Flambeau Field Athletics	10%
Faul Threw Roofing	6%
Left Feet Dance Studio	5%
Self Repair Auto	-4%
Waterless Car Wash	-5%
Left Over Foods	-7%

The next document the team reviewed showed profitability by person. The CFO listed all the employees and their profit dollar contribution to the organization. As the group absorbed the information, I could see those who were at the bottom looking a bit uncomfortable. As I stated, Jim is an incredible team builder and took blame for the lowered numbers. At the same time, he also pushed back on the team to improve performance.

Figure 2 Profits by Person

Amber T Topsales	$85,002
Larry No'Two	$77,312
Ella M. Good	$74,899
Sam T Middleman	$50,189
Manford Halfway	$45,000
Mila Beelow	$15,200
Languid Seller	$1,159
Laston List	-$32,000

He set a series of meetings to change the overall department strategy towards customers. First, his team worked with those folks who had poor performing customers, encouraging them to ask for fee increases. As a result, the organization lost half the lower performing customers, yet raised profitability for the entire group.

For those who were at the lower end of profitability, I conducted special coaching activities with them that helped them realize they were under-charging for their services. One person, for example, saved a homeowner $50,000 in additional work by simply redesigning a driveway and the patio areas. Because he was not an engineer, he felt that he should provide this information free as part of other work that he was doing. As a result, he only charged the homeowner $1800, an insignificant amount of money for substantial savings. I helped him realize that he could have charged for the value of the savings. As I explained, most of us would spend $8000 to $10,000 to save $50,000, $50,000 that we would have to pay ordinarily. He could have returned to the customer, explaining that, "The city would require a $50,000 structure because of his current home design. I can design a change that will cost $10,000 but will eliminate the $50,000 modification. Would you be interested in our approach?"

From all the team effort, the department profitability moved from 10% to 20%, all within less than sixty days. Months later, they still maintain this high level of productivity.

Open Book Management

As the example above illustrates, letting your employees know how their efforts impact the organization provides a powerful performance incentive. I want to tell you about two organizations that have taken the idea of open-book management to heart. The first organization, Tasty Catering, run by Tom Walter and his brothers, performs at the highest levels of any small organization I have ever encountered.

I visited Tasty Catering and was immediately impressed by the incredible feeling of positivity exhibited by everybody I met. I was visiting with a group of colleagues, and the group welcomed us as though we were long-lost family. Each person we met asked us if there was anything we needed to help make our visit more fulfilling.

Tom Walter, with several others, wrote a book called *It's My Company Too*, which explained the enormous success realized by Tom and others of similar mind. I highly recommend you pick up this publication so that you may understand how Tom and his team created such success.

First, let me set the stage regarding the performance of Tasty Catering. The Gallup organization has consistently found that good engagement scores, on average, around 70% worldwide. (As we mentioned earlier, engagement is a leading indicator of improved performance and profitability.) Those organizations who exceed this level are indeed performing well. Tasty Catering, on the other hand, consistently sees their engagement scores at 92% or higher, an astoundingly high score. Tasty Catering employees bring discretionary effort and creativity to work every day, thinking of ways to make the organization more effective, efficient, and profitable. As a result, Tom told our group that his profitability rose by 50% that year. One of his employees, for example, conducted research discovering that gasoline prices are at their lowest on Tuesdays and Wednesdays. By encouraging drivers to fill up the catering trucks on those days, this young man helped save the organization $25,000. This example is just one instance of the creativity that organizations can unleash when employees are fully engaged in a company.

During our visit to Tasty Catering, Tom brought us into their all-purpose room, where we observed a large plastic writable surface that covered the two-story wall of one side of the room. On the surface, were approximately ten expense and profit lines corresponding to the profit and loss accounting for the business. For example, one line contained supplies that the company needed to have on hand to produce meals. Another line spelled out sales targets for the group. Each line was assigned to a team who worked to assure that budget goals were met. In this way, Tom managed his organization through small groups, teams that felt responsible for achieving budget goals. No team would ever feel comfortable letting down their fellow associates.

Nick Sarillo, who wrote a book called a *Piece of the Pie*, runs two large pizza restaurants, which he operates uniquely. During a tour of Nick's restaurant, we walked through his basement, where on the wall, like Tasty Catering, are expense and profit lines for his restaurant. Each line is assigned to a member of his team, and he often assigns employees as young as 16 to manage a profit line. He rotates responsibilities so that each employee learns how to run all profit or expense lines. After cycling through all of the expense lines, employees are equipped to manage a restaurant of their own. A 16-year-old working at Nick's Pizza and Pub, will, within five years, be able to strike out on his or her own to run other foodservice organizations.

Like Tasty Catering, employees bring imagination and enthusiasm to their work, enthusiasm that often results in cost savings. For example, Nick told us that a restaurant of his size would typically have $50,000 in liquor inventory. Because his people are highly engaged and creative, his team was able to decrease inventory to a figure closer to $15,000, significantly reducing cash outflows.

When we toured the kitchen area, Nick showed a group of slotted shelves like those used to hold timecards. The cards, in this case, were red on one side and green on the other. Each card had instructions on how to start up a specific area of the kitchen. When his employees arrived to open, each person would choose one of the cards, which started with their red surface facing outward. Then the employee would perform the task on the card. After completing each task, associates would place the cards back in the slotted shelves showing the greenside facing outward. When all cards showed green, managers could easily understand that the employees had completed all opening processes.

Nick repeated these time-saving and easy-to-use processes across his restaurant. As a result, he required fewer supervisors allowing him to reduce management staff to approximately one-third one would usually see in restaurants of his size.

Deliberate Practice for Expert Performance

Increasing profitability means understanding your business at a detailed level. This chapter was not intended to substitute for proper accounting practices but was to highlight several best practices that have helped companies achieve stellar business outcomes.

To assure that you are getting the most profitability and performance from your employees, do the following:

- Conduct an engagement survey each year to understand your progress. The higher the engagement score, the better the performance of your organization.

- Have your accountant produce monthly reports showing the profitability of each customer and similar performance of each employee. Help your employees to find ways to become more productive.

Are you ready to be more profitable? Assess yourself and understand your growth opportunities at

www.expertperformance.com/be-more-profitable.

CHAPTER 7

LEADING LEADERS

Harness and focus the amazing power of your leadership team

One of my clients has an elaborate, detailed mission and vision statement hung on the walls at the company's various locations. It's large, about 18 inches long and 12 inches wide. The framed statement is hard to miss. Most employees pass by the document every day. Regrettably, longer is not necessarily better.

An unmemorable mission and vision statement often has an unanticipated negative. During a visit to the same client's offices, I asked a group of associates to explain the company's vision and mission. After a brief awkward silence and a few furtive glances, one person cautiously spoke. "I think I read it at some time, but I don't remember it." (It was on the wall behind them.) A few moments passed, and another offered, "I think the real mission is to make money for the owners."

Even though at the time the answer surprised me, thinking back, it made sense. The situation reminded me of one of the great rules of leadership, a rule everyone should remember. **In the absence of information and communication, people will always think the worst.**

We have been hardwired genetically to think the worst of situations when the intentions of others are unknown. Imagine a caveman and woman in their cozy home eating around the fire with their family. A rather large stranger and his group of club-carrying friends walk through the entrance of their cave. If the caveman and woman thought, "Oh joy, they brought clubs to play a game!" that family is no longer in our gene pool! Survival often meant suspicion.

Suspicion arises every day. One of my clients, for example, was left off the list for a meeting that she thought she should have attended, and the perceived slight made her feel marginalized and angry. Rather than stew in her upset, I suggested she consider talking to the organizer to understand why he did not extend an invitation. To my client's surprise, the meeting organizer described his positive intention; he did not want to waste her time since the agenda topics did not directly involve her. I'm sure she felt a rush of relief as my client thanked him for his consideration. She went on to explain that perhaps she might have attended to provide added valuable insight. After more discussion, they agreed that going forward, they would consult one another before each meeting to understand whether my client's attendance would make a significant contribution.

As leaders, we must be vigilant, often offering more communication than we think necessary to help our employees and associates to prevent "thinking the worst."

First, Establish a Powerful Purpose

While working with a hospital, I had the good fortune to talk with one of the cooks. This older gentleman, who grew up in the South and ended his schooling with a sixth-grade education, created dismay among the dietitians with his southern-fried cooking favorites. On his fried chicken days, the hospital grapevine went into overdrive, and shortly after lunch began, lines appeared, food disappeared, and latecomers felt disappointment.

After we built a connection with him, he told us that he believed his job was far more important than those of the medical staff. My colleague and I turned to one another, wondering what this man's rationale could be. As he explained further, we nodded in understanding, "The physicians do their best to make people well, but without my food, they die." Now that is a purpose!

In the absence of a well-defined purpose, organizations suffer from a lack of focused decision making, and employees will work solely for their good and not that of the company. Whenever I observe leaders working to benefit themselves at the exclusion of their organization, I know that a clear and compelling purpose remains unspoken.

When a business has a defined purpose shared among all the leadership and line staff, the company has a true North Star and a single direction on which to rely for decision making. This singular focus shone brightly when I asked associates at one of my clients, who made medical diagnostic machines, to tell me their organization's purpose. To a person, everyone with whom I talked told me that they were in the business of saving lives; every decision, all strategies, and the total of their work centered on this ultimate purpose.

Second, Develop Your Leaders

I had the opportunity to know an extraordinary leader, Tim, at one of my clients. Across his organization, Tim has a reputation for creating a stellar culture that has contributed to one of the most profitable divisions in the organization. One day I asked him his secrets for creating a top organization. He replied with a simple but elegant answer, "You build a great team first. The business will follow." His division, one of the most profitable and well-run in the company, has all but eliminated the competition.

I discovered more about Tim, who has a talent for developing leadership.

First, he apprenticed his underlings, teaching them how to do what he can do–AND how to do it better.

Second, he replaced himself. Over time, Tim developed those underneath to take his job. Today, Tim, who used to oversee the division, is now one of two managing partners. His mentored and coached leaders succeeded him.

Finally, he ensured that his replacement leaders had a complete set of capabilities so that Tim's future interventions would be minimal. When we miss this step, critical situations can derail us and distract us from our primary job. One of my clients leads a division of her company and has several regional leaders reporting to her. One of those leaders had a sticky and difficult customer situation, a situation which required quick resolution. Rather than engage in necessary conflict with the customer, the regional leader allowed the challenge to remain in the hands of one of his local project managers, a project manager who lacked the tools necessary to resolve the issue.

The situation worsened, and the division leader consulted me. After gaining understanding, I advised the leader to intervene directly and to instruct the regional manager how to resolve future challenges. His investigation quickly determined the root cause of the difficulty, and, together with his local leader, he created a plan which quickly resolved the situation. This example illustrates that when a subordinate leader lacks capability, the senior leader will be drawn away from his or her tasks to address incompetency. If you as a leader fail to create high capability among your direct reports, you will have to do their job and yours.

How to Delegate Professionally

When I was employed by IBM, my manager told me how his manager assured that a task his boss delegated was completed. For example, if an assignment was due by 4 o'clock in the afternoon and my boss had not met the deadline, he would receive a follow-up phone call about the delegated activity. His manager also placed a note in my boss' personnel file for consideration at annual salary adjustment time. No one would ever be late more than a single time.

I have the opportunity to talk to many high performing leaders, enabling me to distill the magic formula for professional delegation.

1. **Create Clarity** - The more precise information we as leaders provide, the more likely we will receive what we want from the person to whom we have delegated tasks. Clarity offers a complete understanding of how we know the person to whom we have delegated tasks will be successful.

   Here is an example of the is the wrong way to provide clarity. Imagine receiving an email with the following.

   I want you to create a new onboarding process. I know you've never done anything like this before, so find out if you can locate other examples of proper onboarding. If you have any questions, you can contact me.

   The assignment is vague. There are no explicit requirements.

   I would much rather receive the following instructions.

   I want you to create a new onboarding process. The process should perform the following: First, it should acquaint new employees with our benefits and pay system. Perhaps a webinar or training session will help employees understand this item. Second, you will want to establish opportunities for folks to meet peers, senior, and line leaders. Third, the onboarding process should uncover existing best practices for helping individuals learn their position. You may want to interview those leaders who have low attrition and who successfully bring people on board regularly. The Society of Human Resource Managers may also have best practices on their website. Feel free to take time to do an Internet search to find the top ways to onboard folks. The process for helping people learn their jobs should be fully documented and then construct a plan to train all leaders on the onboarding best practices.

2. **Provide clear end dates. Add check-in conversations if needed.**

Providing a precise due date and time not only ensures success, but such a practice also enables leadership to balance workloads. Once you've assigned a date and time, record the information in your calendar. Doing so helps in two ways. First, you can easily hold folks accountable to the end dates, and second, you can effortlessly discern whether you have assigned too many tasks to one person.

Check-ins. Expert leaders feel reluctance to assign a task and then leave its success to chance. From our work with these leaders, they will assign check-in times when the task meets specific criteria:

- The person performing the task has never performed the activity and will need guidance.
- The task is involved, i.e., it requires multiple steps and often involves others in the organization.
- The task holds a high importance to the organization's success.

Check-ins often allow employees to struggle a bit without having them feel failure. We want our reports and colleagues to persevere even under adverse conditions and to feel successful, that their efforts have been worthwhile.

I was working with an executive who was fond of having people make mistakes so they would "learn." Unfortunately, after assigning a task, he would wait until the project was completed to inform the person that he or she had traveled the wrong road, failing the assignment. Then, he would offer corrections and have the person repeat the task. In the executive's mind, his approach helped people to learn from their mistakes. In actuality, this executive was frustrating his people, wasting time, and expending valuable organizational resources. The frustration his people felt diminished their learning capacity and decelerated their knowledge acquisition.

Following is the wrong way to provide an end date.

As I mentioned, I want you to work on an onboarding process. The task might take you 4 to 6 weeks. Please let me know when you have reached completion.

The end date is vague and leaves the completion of the project up to the associate. Unfortunately, the employee often has the least knowledge about the importance and priority of the delegated tasks. Leaving completion decisions to associates often leads to poor organizational performance.

Here is the right way to provide end dates and check-ins.

As I mentioned, I want you to create a new onboarding process. This assignment is due the 15th of next month by the end of the day. Once we have reviewed your findings and recommendations, I'll have you present to the rest of the leadership team. Since this task is a challenging and complicated activity, we will have weekly milestone check-ins so that we are both assured that you are successful. On Friday of next week at our usual meeting at 2 PM, I would like to hear what you have learned about the best onboarding practices. At the end of each session, we will set an agenda for our next weekly check-in.

3. Hold each other accountable

   To round out one's ability to delegate effectively, you will want to hold religiously to your negotiated end dates. As I mentioned earlier, the best managers will write check-in and end dates on their calendar then immediately follow up when the manager does not meet expectations. This follow-up educates your staff that due dates are serious. I worked with many managers who allow completion assignments to slip merely because they became too busy and failed to hold the leader accountable to agreed-upon dates.

   One of my clients complained to me that she was not moving her group along quickly enough. Her leaders, she explained, often did not produce results on time. As our discussions progressed, we discovered that she often failed to provide clear outcomes and

> deadlines. Conflicting work, such as client projects, often displaced tasks that she assigned, and she allowed noncompliance behavior to continue because she understood that customer work brought in revenue. However, even though the team performed well, she could not move her department to the outcomes she needed. We worked together to create clarity and precise deadlines. As a result, her organization gained new business and increased profitability.

If managers delegate incorrectly, they can find themselves becoming inefficient and fail to achieve goals. When I first joined IBM, managers would talk about not letting the monkey climb on their back. This brilliant metaphor illustrates a common issue. Employees have a fondness for allowing their bosses to take on tasks that should have remained in the employee's capable hands. The monkey is now on the boss's back. Many new managers make this mistake, readily agreeing to do the employee's work, resulting in lowered effectiveness. Leaders found the best alternative is to follow the delegation process above.

Know When to Intervene

One of my clients, Jacob, had a very sticky, complicated, and challenging issue occur. One of his managers, John, two levels down in the organization was having difficulty providing clear direction to his team, causing rework and frustration. The situation deteriorated so severely that several of John's direct reports complained to HR. Then, HR became sufficiently alarmed to talk to John's manager and Jacob's direct report, Charlotte, explaining the situation and reviewing the complaints.

Charlotte then spoke to John. Since HR's conversations included employees only, Charlotte had heard second hand only one side of the story. As a result, Charlotte's talk with John stirred trust issues between the two of them. John felt isolated.

As you can readily understand, the incident became more and more intertwined, complicated, and with numerous communication pathways. When multiple parties become involved, in this case three levels of management, employees and HR, we as leaders must cut through the noise then find and repair the root cause of the distress.

At this point, I spoke with Jacob, recommending that he intervene personally to discover the ins and outs of this situation to understand all sides of the issue.

After a few interviews, Jacob understood the root cause of the frustrations and rework. John's communication style felt too direct, and his reports often felt intimidated, making them reluctant to ask clarifying questions. Armed with the additional information, he and I devised a plan to coach John how to interact more effectively with his team. Within a short period, the team frustration subsided, and the team stabilized.

Problematic and difficult situations require that the leader gain fuller insight through interventions. Usually, these interventions take the form of interviews or, in more complicated cases, real-time observations. These two interventional approaches enable us as leaders to identify the real causes of problems and challenges. Once we understand the fundamental reasons behind issues and challenges, solutions become apparent.

Often, we as leaders fail to intervene with our team when we should. The following are a few guidelines to help you as a leader know when to.

- An issue has led to an unwanted outcome and seems to defy solution. If a problem occurs, whether technical or interpersonal, you will need to intervene.

- Poor performance, again leading to unwanted outcomes, presents another reason for intervention.

- More often than we would care to admit, we may have leaders who are incompetent in one or more aspects of their job. Incompetency can occur for several reasons: 1) the individual may be new to the position, 2) the individual may have a blind spot or has never encountered a similar situation, or 3) the problem or issue is complex and requires the contribution of multiple individuals. Any of these situations can prevent the team from reaching its goals, requiring involvement on your part.

As I mentioned earlier, each time a leader intervenes with his or her direct reports, that leader experiences loss of significant amounts of time, time that could be used to further the goals of the company.

Failure to intervene can have even more severe consequences. In the example above, before Jacob decided to intervene directly, he wasted almost three person-days while he was involved in unproductive discussions with HR and his direct report. His direct intervention took only a few hours. Had he intervened earlier, he would have saved himself several days of unnecessary effort and discomfort.

The Value of the A Team

One of my clients and friends, Noah, works for a real estate outsourcing firm. His organization gave Noah the responsibility for the outsourcing facilities management for a new client, a large banking organization. The bank had high-performance expectations that Noah had to deliver by the end of the first year, expectations that would translate to a significant monetary reward for him, his team, and his organization. Noah had little time to establish the effective processes that would produce required results. His team had to be top-notch from the first day. Unfortunately, he had to hire several of the customer's employees who then become Noah's company employees.

From the first day, he knew that several of these new employees would be unable to produce needed results.

As a side note, many organizations have compassion for people who do not have the capabilities they may need for their leadership position. Instead, these companies willingly spend resources on raising skills of their people, giving them multiple chances to produce. One of my clients, who has been enormously successful, does just that. Providing these growth resources has become a staple of their culture.

There is a big BUT. **Every day that you do not have the A-Team in place, you reduce overall performance or slip another day from your goals**.

Noah knew that he had very little time for his team to reach the high goals set by the banking organization, nor did he have time to grow people who did not have the required capabilities and competencies. He quickly replaced these individuals with high performers. He had his A-Team. By the end of the year, he exceeded the bank's expectations.

If you don't have a top-performing team reporting to you, you have several choices:

1. You can replace low performers on your team. You may have to pay more for these individuals, but the extra money may be worth it.

2. Many organizations cannot afford A players or even find them. Instead, you will need to frequently intervene and train the B players until they reach A levels. As mentioned in a previous chapter, a clear path for development and training ensures that these individuals reach full capabilities.

Deliberate Practice for Expert Performance

- Work with your leadership team to create a clear, concise, and easy to remember purpose for the organization and make sure that everyone on your team supports that purpose. Ensure that your entire organization uses the purpose as a guiding light for activities and decision-making.

- Develop the leaders underneath you so that they can take your place.

- Professionally delegate to your team.

- Intervene when those reporting to you have challenges or issues that prevent your organization from reaching its goals.

- Assure that you have an A-Team reporting to you; otherwise, you will have to do their work as well as yours.

Are you ready to lead leaders? Assess yourself and understand your growth opportunities at www.expertperformance.com/Leading-leaders.

CHAPTER 8

THE POWER OF INFLUENCE

Sharpen the essential tools that move others to action and results

From our research, the primary tool each leader must have is the ability to influence others. Top-performing leaders exercise a masterful ability to persuade their people and colleagues to take action. Noticing this phenomenon, my colleague, Cindy Riehman, who at the time worked for Dade Behring (now part of Siemens), and I began a research project to understand how a few individuals could make such an impact on others. We created an Expert Performance Success Map™ of those who the organization had recognized as having extraordinary influencing skills.

Our study showed that their influence centered on three areas:

1. An ability to build trust and credibility

2 A capability to appeal to other's motivations

3. A competence to execute their work

From the results of this study, we created a one day Influencing Without Authority workshop to help individuals in various organizations to become highly persuasive. The following paragraphs explain each of the areas listed above.

One of my clients who I mentioned earlier, Tim, gave me a lesson in building trust and credibility. I was one of several consultants invited to an anniversary celebration of my client's organization. My wife and I moved slowly through the crowd of 400 people to find our assigned seating. To my surprise, I was seated at the front table with the two managing principals. When I saw Tim, one of the principals, I stood to walk around the table to greet him. Instead, Tim told me to remain seated, and he would come to me. I'll never forget this lesson in humbleness and graciousness, two characteristics I found consistently in great leaders, leaders who build strong trust and credibility with others. Be humble, be gracious, because even the most commanding leaders run an organization through the commitment of others.

Tim is a trust builder. He has mastered what we have found to be the six critical skills for building trust and credibility. The six components are:

1. Frequent use of reflective language
2. Regular practice of empathic language
3. Framing of issues
4. The reframing of tough or challenging problems
5. Embracing and using defensiveness of others
6. Ability to give negative feedback.

Reflective language.

Early in my IBM career, I had difficulty with one of my managers making my position particularly challenging. He had high expectations of me, but because I was new, I did not have the competency to achieve desired results. Sleep became elusive, and I would frequently wake worried about my job. Life took a sharp turn in a downward direction. Although I would not admit it, I experienced symptoms of mild depression. My wife is a psychologist, so I was naturally inclined to seek help from a mental health professional. Unfortunately, my wife's recommendation had no openings, so she recommended another psychologist who was early in his practice.

The first (and last) visit did not go well. The day of the appointment arrived, and I anxiously looked forward to relief from my symptoms. I made myself comfortable and began to explain my situation. For the next few minutes, I told my story. "I was having trouble sleeping," I said. "I felt sad, and was not finding much joy in life." After a short pause, the therapist responded (I think with a bit of triumph at the discovery of a diagnosis), " Oh, you are depressed!" I was stunned. I rebutted emphatically, "No, not depressed!

I *am* having trouble sleeping. Life is devoid of joy." Once again he pronounced his diagnosis. I was definitely depressed, he said.

The word *depressed* never came from my lips. Looking back, I realize that the therapist correctly concluded that I was depressed, but I did not want to hear that word. The diagnosis deeply offended me, and I never returned.

Moral of the story: When talking with other people about difficult issues, use *their* words in the conversation. Speaking your words assumes your words are equivalent to theirs, and if you are mistaken, you will likely disrupt connection instantly.

Instead, employ reflective language. Reflective language delivers the words and phrases of the other person back to him or her. Using reflective language lets others know you are listening and builds a secure connection.

Here are several examples:

Example 1

Other person: I had a run-in with my boss today. She was in a foul mood and just seemed as though she could not listen to me.

You: You had a run-in with your boss today? (By using their words, you have let the other person know that you are listening.)

Example 2

Other person: I am upset with the way you've handled this sale to our company.

You: If I understand correctly, you are upset with the way with I handled the sale to your company. Tell me more so that I can understand what happened. (You have let the person know that you are listening as well as demonstrating care for the other person's perceptions. This technique is an excellent way to reduce conflict.)

Example 3 – How NOT to do reflective listening

Other person: I had a run-in with my boss today. She was in a foul mood and just seemed as though she could not listen.

You: I suggest you go back in to tell your boss that she needs to take a minute to listen to you. (Probably the biggest listening mistake most of us make is trying to solve the other person's problem. Most of us can solve our problems once we feel calm. A calm state of mind releases the resources to address those challenges.)

Empathic Language

Once we have built a connection through several instances using reflective listening, we may be able to offer an empathic response. Empathic statements use feeling words to identify the emotions behind the words and tend to build a deeper connection. Once you make a deeper connection, you have more opportunities to influence. We must be careful to avoid mislabeling the emotion which would break the connection with the other person. However, I found that reflective listening used for the first few minutes builds a secure connection, and if you do miss the precise feeling, there is often willingness by the other person to help you identify a better equivalent.

Here are several examples.

Example

Other person: I had a run-in with my boss today. She was in a foul mood and just seemed as though she could not listen to me.

You: You had a run-in with your boss today? I'm sorry to hear that. Seems like she was in a foul mood. (This is an example of two reflective language statements.)

Other person: Yes, I had terrific ideas that she dismissed.

You: So In addition to not listening to you, she dismissed your ideas (two more examples of reflective listening).

Other person: Yeah, I got out of there as fast as I could. That'll be about the last time I bring new ideas to her.

You: That whole situation must have been pretty annoying and from what you've told me you were pretty ticked. (This is the first opportunity to use empathic language - annoying and ticked.)

Other person: Yep, I was pretty angry about the situation (the person has opened up to precisely how they felt-angry).

Empathic language provides an excellent opportunity to demonstrate that you not only heard what was said, you also exhibit compassion and caring. Such behavior will help you to enhance your connection to the other person.

Framing - how to make even the most negative feedback acceptable

I was in the Art Institute of Chicago standing in front of a magnificent picture painted by a master artist. The colors were glorious and the craftsmanship superb. As I paused a moment taking in the beauty, I felt a small but growing uneasiness. A few more moments passed until I became fully aware of the troubling feeling. It was the frame, which seemed awkwardly out of place and detracted from the artist's beautiful work. Beautiful frames enclosed other paintings nearby, enhancing their beauty. The change of a frame, I thought to myself, makes the difference between a stunning piece and one less so.

Just as in art, we can use *word framing* to help individuals to become aware of the positive side of a situation. The other day I was meeting with a new client, an owner of a small business. He described a moderately performing employee who was not setting any work speed records. As a small business owner, a single employee can mean the difference between profitability and loss. I suggested using several objective measures to help understand the person's capabilities and potential. The owner felt concern that if he told the employee he needed coaching, the employee might be offended.

I suggested word framing. Just as in art, word framing can cause a negative message to be perceived positively.

Let me give you an example of the wrong way to do word framing. How would you like to have your boss say this to you? (This is a real-life example.)

Owner: Jim, your performance has not been at a level we find acceptable. In fact, your work is pretty average. We want you to take a couple of assessments to find out where your challenges are and see if we can correct them.

Employee: I had no idea you were dissatisfied.

Owner: Now you know.

Here is the right way to frame. (I told my client to take the following approach.)

Owner: Jim, we value you here and want to invest in your success. I have a colleague and friend who is an excellent coach, and we would like you to work with him. Your success is as vital to us as it is to you. He'll send you several links to assessments, and then we'll understand what your most substantial capabilities are and how we can maximize those.

Employee: That sounds terrific. There are several areas in which I feel like I could use the help. Let's get started.

I received an email from Jim written precisely this way: I'M EXCITED!

Framing is a powerful tool to help set expectations for the message that you plan to deliver. It builds connection with others, allowing you to be more influential. Framing is an excellent way to position negative feedback and to show our intent is to help the individual improve.

Reframing:

My good friend Tom believed that staying in shape was essential to his health and had been an avid exerciser all his life. His current health club was closing, so he needed to find a new gym. He chose a club near his house that, because it had affiliated with a hospital, required a physical examination before joining. Tom scheduled his physical, which proceeded normally except for an electrocardiogram which showed slight anomalies. The doctor suggested to Tom that the anomalies did not appear severe but scheduled a stress test anyway to rule out any issues. The stress test went as planned, with Tom reaching the highest levels, but again the doctor found anomalies which he thought were suspicious but not severe. The Doctor told Tom that to be safe, he should undergo an angiogram which would provide definitive results, letting Tom know whether he had heart blockages.

The tests showed unexpected results: blockages in four arteries, including a 90% blockage in the widow maker artery. The actual clots themselves were no thicker than a dime, yet could have had devastating consequences if untreated. He was not allowed to go home from the hospital and was immediately scheduled for surgery the next morning. I visited him the day before his operation.

Tom told me that he felt terrible because he had exercised regularly his entire life and now he was a heart patient. I could see the discouragement. I thought for a moment then said, "Tom, if you had not been serious about your exercise, you would not have joined a new health club, taken the physical followed by multiple tests. You likely would not have survived. It was your dedication to physical fitness that's going to keep you alive." I could see Tom thinking for a moment. Then realizing his dedication to exercise, as he had planned, was going to bring him a longer life, he nodded in agreement.

I tell you this story to illustrate the power of reframes. Reframing, as the name suggests, takes what is usually a negative situation, a frame, and replaces it with a new and more positive frame. The new frame allows a person to understand the situation from another perspective. In this case, Tom felt terrible that, even though he had exercised his entire life, he was still a heart patient. I reframed the situation so that Tom understood that had he not been someone who exercised regularly, he likely would not have survived.

Example:

Linda: I spent all evening completing the Baker report because I thought our boss needed it at 8 o'clock this morning. When I arrived at 7:30, she told me that last night the meeting had been postponed until tomorrow. That sure is annoying since I worked so hard.

You: (Begin with reflective and empathic language.) Wow, you spent all evening getting ready for a meeting that's not happening until tomorrow. I can see how annoyed you are since she knew last night that the meeting had been postponed.

Linda: Yes, I wish she would've called.

You: That sure would've been nice had she called. Well, (here's the reframe) at least your work is done, and the report is complete. You can take that off your mind and do something that is more productive.

Linda: Yes, I wish she would've called, but you are right. At least the report is complete.

Reframing enables us to help another person understand the situation from a different perspective. Sometimes situations are heavily emotion-laden, and sometimes not. Either way, reframing creates strong connection and allows you to have significant influence.

Stop Fighting Resistance

I was working with one of my clients, who is a CEO of a medical research society. Her organization raises money to help fund new and promising treatments for a type of cancer that has, in the past, been fatal. As its leader, her organization requires her to speak frequently. She complained that she did not always feel confident and comfortable as a speaker. Since I am a professional speaker and enjoy speaking in front of groups, I felt well equipped to help and began to offer her what I thought was extraordinary expertise. I reminded her to tell stories and engage emotions. No matter what audience sits before you, involve them in the joy you experience every day in your position.

Sounds great? Right on target. Even though I could see that she was trying to make changes, I could tell that her heart was not in it. With each suggestion, I could hear the tacit, "Yes, buts." "Yes, but that's not the audience that I have every time," she would say. "I want to tell the right stories and deliver the best message for each group." At every suggestion, I found a small but graciously expressed speedbump.

Finally, I realized that I was trying to teach her *my* speaking methods. She was stumbling, and I was trying to rescue her! I needed a different approach.

I thought of my friend, David Massello (an excellent coach), who introduced me to the work of Milton Erikson. A master of short-term therapy, Dr. Erikson could identify the resources a person used in one aspect of their lives then redirect that resource to better themselves in a different part. I was about to find the key to my client's success.

At the next session, I asked her about a time she felt extremely confident, a key indicator of her success. As she recalled the event, she talked of the in-depth preparation she made before the speech that assured herself and her audience that the talk was engaging, accurate, and spoke directly to her listeners.

Herein lies the rub. She believed that she needed to understand the audience make-up before each speech. However, she sometimes had to speak to audiences whose make up was unknown to her, which prevented her from preparing ahead, causing her to feel on edge and ill at ease.

In general, "How many types of people do you speak to," I asked. She thought for a moment, then responded that there were three groups, and all could be in the same audience.

As a side note, when we prepare thoroughly and practice to become capable and competent, we naturally perform more effectively. All professionals practice, whether they are physicians, pilots, athletes, artists or speakers. They all prepare fully.

I responded to my client that she had solved her problem. I reminded her that she only felt confident when fully prepared. She nodded in agreement. Well, you just need to prepare three speeches so when you do not know the make-up of the audience beforehand, you can attend the meeting, ask who is present – through conversations before the session or a show of hands – then give the speech for that group, one of the speeches you prepared ahead of time.

In a moment, acknowledgment registered on her face. "That's a good idea," she replied. "I could prepare and be ready for about anything."

Her resources solved the problem and made her a much more confident and capable speaker.

Many times, leaders find themselves in opposition to a staff person and experience arguments or silent resistance. If we view resistance as an attempt by the other person to express an opinion or a disagreement, we do not have to become upset or confrontational. Instead, we invite you to use a technique demonstrated in the story above – embracing resistance instead of fighting it.

Here are the steps:	Example:
Use reflective listening to let the other person know you understand.	You: I know you will be an excellent leader and make a difference in this organization. I think you need to step up and take the role. Other person: I'm not so sure that I can do this. You: So you're not sure that you can step up to the new role?
Employ empathic listening to deepen the connection so that the other person feels less confrontational and more engaged in your conversation.	Other person: Yes, that's correct. I've been able to run my practice, but that's different than running the entire division. You: From what you're saying, you seem to be a bit concerned about taking a bigger leadership role. Other person: Yes, I don't know if I can do it.
Make sure that you understand the issue.	You: What stands in your way? Other person: I've never done a role like this before, and the previous leader had such an impact. I'm not sure I can fill her shoes.
Help the individual discover resources in other aspects of his or her life that can be used in the current situation.	You: I want you to think about times when you were asked to lead other groups in your past. Other person: Well, I've been asked to lead just about every organization I've been in. In college, I was asked to be the president of my sorority. All through my work, people asked me to lead different efforts. You: If I understand you correctly, you have been asked to run many different organizations and efforts. Is that correct? Other person: Yes, that's correct. You: Have you been successful in these engagements? If so, how did you know what to do? Other person: Well, I used to make a list before I started the new job of all the things that I needed to accomplish and know. I would start working on that list right away.
Help the person use the new resource in the current situation.	You: What if you were to do the same process in this situation. Make your list and begin to discover what you need to know and learn. Other person: Yes, that makes a lot of sense. I think I could get started on this right away.

Appeal to the motivations of others

I had the opportunity to coach a young man who was working for a large credit card company. Kyle was relatively new to the organization and had not had much exposure to the more successful sales representatives with whom he worked. He was concerned because he was reaching only 50%

of his quota and the year continued to slip by. He watched the more experienced employee in the territory next to him receive a demotion and pay cut because he had not reached his sales goals. Kyle was worried and did not know what to do.

We had produced an Expert Performance Success Map™ of top-performing salespeople in Kyle's organization. We compared Kyle to these high-performing individuals so that we could understand what my client needed to do to achieve successful outcomes. (I explain how to capture expertise in a later chapter.)

We can tell people how to improve, but unless they feel the motivation to do so, we will find our efforts derailed.

The first activity we conducted with Kyle uncovered his motivation. After asking Kyle the question, "What is important you personally in your work?" (This question always elicits a person's motivation), Kyle explained that providing for his family was his number one motivation. If he were to have his salary reduced, he would be unable to pay his mortgage and provide food for his wife and children. Indeed, this was strong motivation!

We discovered that Kyle was only calling on ten clients per week, but to achieve his goals, he needed to talk to thirty. At first, Kyle was skeptical that he would be able to triple his work. Once we explained that if Kyle were to call on customers in a geographic location, he could reduce travel time by enough to call on the thirty clients.

Finally, we asked Kyle the question, "Do you understand how calling on additional clients will increase your performance enough to provide for your family?" He responded with an enthusiastic yes. Kyle continued his hard work, doubling his sales in ninety days and tripling them in the next ninety. At the beginning of the following year, he received a promotion.

The story above illustrates the uncovering and connection of motivation to what we need a person to do to perform well.

Here are the steps and an example.

Steps	Example
Ask the person, "What is important to you personally in your work?"	Other person: It's important to me to please the customer.
Ask, "What else is personally important to you and your work?"	Other person: I like to be accurate.
Continue asking, "What else is important to you personally in your work?" until the person repeats or ends.	Other person: I think that's about it.
Ask, "If you have all those things that you mentioned, what will they do for you?" (You are listening for big concept words like satisfaction, fulfillment, or enjoyment.)	Other person: I feel satisfied.
If you have a project or an activity which you want the other person to engage in, you can tie the activity back to the other person's motivation.	You: I have a project that will please a lot of customers. Would you be interested in participating? (Because the person had mentioned the importance of pleasing customers, we tie the project directly back to the individual's motivation.)

Sometimes, thinking about what a person does not say is as important as what they do. In the example above, the individual does not mention that relationships are essential. Pleasing the customer, yes, but building collaboration with coworkers was not mentioned. If you need an individual to be a team player, and you did not hear a collaborative motivation, the person may not be a good fit for your organization.

Flawless Execution

We have found that flawless execution, which has four elements, makes a substantial contribution to top performance. The elements are:

1. Use of specific language
2. Positive language
3. Future-paced language
4. Removing barriers

Specific Language

When I worked for IBM, I had a terrific boss named Ted, who supported all of his team and made our jobs fun. During one of my performance reviews, Ted asked me to communicate better with him. I liked Ted, wanted to please him, so after leaving my meeting with him, I thought of several ways to improve my communication. I settled on an elaborate report given to him each Monday detailing everything I did the previous week. If I say so, I produced a thing of beauty. For several weeks, I labored over the format, giving him an even better version of what I thought was essential information. I assumed he could hardly wait until Monday afternoon to read my latest installment. I bet you can imagine what happened next. Ted, the ever-mindful diplomat, said, "Vince, I appreciate the hard work you put into communication with me, but all I want is a brief phone call each week." Upon hearing this, I should have been relieved because I didn't have to work so hard and could capture considerable time to do something more substantial. I guess I felt a small amount of disappointment, though, because my beautiful work had, in reality, overwhelmed him with too much data. I eventually got over it once I realized I had learned a valuable lesson.

We tend to use the word communication frequently, making it one of the most unspecified words heard in business conversations. The word *communication* is not specific language, i.e., it does not describe what we see, feel, hear, touch, taste, and smell when we have good communication. Ted used this unspecified word, communication, leaving me to sharpen the meaning, causing me to inadvertently define communication in a way that mismatched Ted's meaning. I should have asked Ted for his specific requirements, which would have created a more productive working relationship. Lesson learned!

Here is an example. Try to find the unspecified words.

(How not to communicate using specific language) You need to communicate more effectively.	This phrase has at least two unspecified words. The first and most apparent is *communicate*, and the second is *effectively*. Neither term tells us precisely what we need to do.
(An example of specific language) I need you to communicate in a way that lets me know how you are spending your work time. I need to know the projects you are working on and the time spent on each. Please give me this information verbally each Monday at 4 o'clock.	These sentences provide a precise instruction set. Notice the clarity and specificity.

Positive Language

When I work with groups of people, I offer this fun exercise. Try it.

I want you to NOT think of pink elephants in tutus dancing. Got it?

How successful were you? I bet you made a beautiful dancing elephant movie in your head. I would wager that you even added music.

Over eons, our brains have been hardwired to make visual representations of what we hear. When we hear a negative, such as the one in this exercise (do not think of pink elephants), we have to take an extra mental step to negate the image we have created. It's as though we first have to make the movie, then put a big red circle with a slash through to account for the word NOT. By then, it's too late. We've already had the thought. How many of us as parents witnessed spilled milk immediately after we had told our child, "Don't spill your milk!" Or perhaps told our little ones "Don't cross the street without me!" only to see our child running gleefully to the other side of the street.

In business, we frequently make similar statements. For example, after a problematic performance review, I've heard managers say, "I know you had a bad performance review. Don't worry." Unfortunately, worrying becomes precisely what we do. Here is another example, "I don't want you to make any more mistakes in your reporting." Our mind becomes filled with pictures of error-ridden documents.

Instead, we want to use positive language, telling others what we want instead of what we don't want. Consider this. "I know we had a difficult performance review. I'd like you to remember that I'm okay with where you are. I know you will continue to improve." Another example: "I hope to see your next report will be exceptional." Both of these examples help us to create a positive, future-oriented image.

To change a phrase from negative to positive, listen for critical phrases or for contractions made from the word *not* such as can't, shouldn't, and won't. Replace the words or phrases with what you want in the future instead. Following are a few more examples.

Negative example	Positive example
I notice you are frequently late for work.	I would like you to work very hard to come in on time to the office.
Your communication skills are lacking.	Let's work together to grow your communication skills.
Please stop complaining and do your job.	I want to hear your concerns as well as watch you excel at your job.

Future Language

Together with positive language, future language can mean the difference between discouragement and inspiration. I worked with a business owner who found the downside in every action taken by his people. He consistently complained about past mistakes. One day, his best salesperson, Terry, walked into the office. Terry's whole body radiated pride and excitement. "Guess what. I just signed up the XYZ company. I've been working on them for the last year, and they finally said yes!" His boss failed to register even the smallest amount of enthusiasm, and Terry's excitement ebbed because he knew what would come next. Martin, who was the owner, complained, "I know you gave up too much. At what price did you sign him up?" Terry, who thought his price was a win for both his company and his customer, answered reluctantly.

"Terry," Martin scoffed, "Haven't I taught you anything? When will you learn? You left money in the deal that should have been ours. You've done this before, and I was hoping you would have learned."

After a few feeble excuses and utterances, Terry walked away dejected, finally realizing that he needed to find another position.

Let's examine a better way to handle Terry's success. Martin could have responded this way.

"Terry, congratulations on your big win. I know you have been chasing this deal for a while, and it must feel terrific."

"Thank you, Martin. I do feel great about the win," responded Terry.

Martin inquired, "What was the price you came in on?" Terry proudly answered. Without a hint of disapproval, Martin would say, "That's great. You got a deal that makes sense for both our company and the client's."

"I think so," replied Terry, who noticed Martin's thoughtful look. "Do you have any suggestions?"

Martin paused for a moment then said, "I like what you did, and you will be even more successful in the future. I'm going to show you a way to maximize our deals, create a win-win for the customer, and put more commission in your pocket. You okay with that?"

"Sure, that sounds terrific," Terry answered.

"Great, come to my office tomorrow morning, and we'll get started."

Notice Martin's statement, "You will be even more successful in the future." Such phrasing causes recipients to place themselves in the future, generating feelings of hope and opportunity. Conversations that regularly bring up past mistakes cause us to turn off creative thinking and instead to expend effort to defend our actions. Every great leader I have interviewed and worked with uses future phrasing, words that inspire, give hope, and direction. Here are a few more examples.

Past: You made a mistake with the client by disagreeing with his request.	Future: I would like to offer several thoughts on how you might handle clients who disagree with you.
Past: You missed your quota last year.	Future: This year, you'll reach your quota. We'll work together to make that happen.

Make Others' Jobs Easier

Jack, one of my customers, complained that he spends 30% of his time following up with others regarding requests for information or reports. "Just the other day," he said, "I asked for a report from Darlene. I know she means well, but I struggle to get things from her."

"What did you do," I inquired.

"First I sent an email saying that I needed the report by Friday of next week. Several days passed, so I followed up. She said she didn't see the email because it was buried with hundreds of others, and she apologized." She told me, "I'll get on it right away."

"Friday morning, I sent another email. Again, no response. So, I sent another one in the afternoon. She finally answered."

She wrote back, "Sorry, my boss put me on a special project, and I had to push your report back."

Jack sighed, "I finally got the report on Monday. My customer was so annoyed, I am going to have to do a lot of rebuilding of trust."

Does this description seem familiar?

To be influential, we can make our jobs and those of colleagues much more manageable by giving them the tools and information they need for success.

When making requests of others, here is what is needed:

- Explain to the other person the importance of the request, preferably in writing. I suggest following with a phone call. Use the email subject header to flag your request as urgent or essential. Assure that the request was received and acknowledged.

- Offer a specific due date, explaining why the date is important. Confirm the timeframe as reasonable.

- Provide necessary tools and information without doing the work yourself. Point the colleague in the right direction.

- Set an agreed-upon follow-up time BEFORE the project is due.

- Ask that your colleague inform you of any unavoidable delays.
- I cannot stress this enough: show appreciation. Thank the person as well as cite the attribute that makes the other person valuable to you.

Here is an example between two colleagues. First the wrong way:

You: I need the budget forecast for the new account by Friday.	Other: I'll get it to you.
Monday arrives. You: It's Monday and I still don't have the analysis	Other: Sorry I didn't get it to you. I had trouble locating the spreadsheet template we use. Then I had difficulty finding the data. In the middle of the project with you, my boss gave me a short assignment. I'll get it to you by day's end.
Here is a better way:	
You: (You will want to send an email and follow with a phone confirmation.) The customer asked me for a budget forecast for their board meeting on the following Tuesday, so I need to get the report from you by Friday. You can find the template you will need on the D drive in the analytics folder. It is titled Budget Forecast. You can get the data from the lead salesperson. He put the original plans together and has a spreadsheet. Are you available Wednesday for a check-in to find out if you have any questions or challenges? Feel free to call me any time.	Other: Thanks for the information and location of the data. That helps. I'll check with my boss to learn whether we have any upcoming projects. Wednesday at 9 am is an excellent time for a status report. I hope that works for you. I'll keep you posted.
Monday arrives. You: Thank you for getting the report to me on Friday. It is great, as usual. You always do terrific work.	Other: You made it easy by helping me understand deadlines as well as to locate the tools and information I needed. Our boss asked me to do a small project, but when I explained the situation, he said I could work on it after I completed the forecast for you.

We increase our influence when we make others' jobs easier and show appreciation.

Conflict Resolution

The leader of a group in one of my clients huffed into the room. We were about to start an Expert Performance Success session. The group included Germans and American associates. "I can't believe the home office in Germany has dictated our procedures without consulting us," said the leader. "We'll lose money if we do it their way." With force in his voice, he explained because of US laws, the new processes would increase departmental US liabilities. The conversation poured over into the workshop, where the Germans patiently explained to the leader, "The decision was made. Nothing can be done."

The leader continued to argue his point while the Germans strongly affirmed he had no recourse but to obey the headquarters edict.

From the team, I found out that when leadership in Germany makes a decision, everyone feels culturally bound to follow that decision. In the US, we might argue with a decision, even to the point of rebellion.

As the meeting progressed, I suggested a way that the team could obey the headquarters directive yet still take advantage of US law. The German directive stipulated a course of action, but the course was vague on the details of how the US should implement the rules. This lack of specificity left the US team with an opening to take advantage of favorable US regulations while complying with German headquarters. A win-win for everyone.

Conflict styles

To understand your conflict styles, I highly recommend the Thomas Kilmann Inventory (TKI) which assesses individuals on five simple-to-understand conflict styles. Please refer to the TKI website for more detail and assessment orders (https://kilmanndiagnostics.com). Here is a summary of suggested styles summarized from Thomas-Kilmann Conflict Mode Instrument.

What	Description	When to use	Example
Competitive – I win, and you don't	Low cooperation and high assertiveness	When something MUST be done	A crisis occurs, and the leader must take charge
Collaborative – win-win	High cooperation and high assertiveness	When there is time for creativity	The organization got a price increase and the customer received more service
Compromise – both parties get something and lose something	Moderate cooperation and moderate assertiveness	Often used when we can't find a win-win solution	Labor negotiation
Accommodation	High cooperation and low assertiveness	Use when one party does not mind the other party getting what it wants	A customer wants more service, and the vendor can provide it without increased cost
Avoidance	Low cooperation and low assertiveness	When giving the situation time to unfold, avoidances provides an advantage	A hot argument between parties who need time to cool

Cultural issues can make a difference in conflict resolution. In the same workshop I mentioned above after I described the collaboration style, which creates a win-win solution for both parties, one of the German participants offered a comment. "In German, we don't have a word for win-win solutions (collaborative style), only a description for good compromise – each group gains and loses something." This explanation, coupled with the previously discussed comments on compliance, enabled the American team members to gain more flexibility to deal with internal team conflict.

From my work with Expert Leaders, I offer the best practices for dealing with conflict.

Here are the steps with examples.

First, seek to understand (see reflective and empathic language). Validate the other person's concerns.	Other: I want to work from home. Other companies do that. It would make a difference for me. You: If I understand, you want to work from home since others do that. Doing so will make a difference. Am I correct? Other: Yes, that's right.
Understand the person's motivations.	You: What's important to you about working from home? Other: I have a long commute and spending more time with my family is a priority. You: I understand. Your family time is important.
Respectfully explain your position.	You: At this time, we have no policies that allow people to work at home. Other: I see. Are there any exceptions?
Determine your conflict style. Compromise or Collaboration is often the most effective. Sometimes competitive is necessary when you cannot break the rules.	
Build an agreement frame. An agreement frame works particularly well with both the compromise and collaboration styles. Agreement frames seek to help the other person achieve what is important to him or her while still holding to what we value.	You: I would like to find a way to help you spend more time with your family while meeting the needs of our company. If I could find a way to help you, would you be willing to help us? Other: Yes, I would. You: In talking to HR, they are afraid of setting a precedent which would allow individuals to work at home. You are a highly valued employee. Since you would like to spend more time with your family, we would like to offer you a flexible start time so that you may spend more time at home in the morning or evening. Will this work for you? Other: I know this is not ideal for me, but it sure helps me spend more time with my family when I need to. Thank you.

Appreciation

Recently, I worked with a client who had an employee who was feeling down and underappreciated. She found herself in a business in which she not only had to sell her work, she had to execute it. In previous jobs, she provided creative services only. Now, she struggled when she added sales and technical tasks. When I first saw her, I could tell she was carrying a burden. One of the instruments I use is Strengthfinder 2.0 from the

Gallup organization. The assessment uncovers the top five strengths of an individual, enabling people to put their energies into activities that are their strong suit.

With my client, I walked through each of her strengths. As we discussed each positive characteristic, I would say things like, "You are probably very good at working with people. I'm sure your customers and colleagues greatly appreciate this characteristic." I could see from the expression on her face that she had lightened up and had begun to replace the "down" feeling with a lighter mood.

Showing appreciation can have a powerful impact on your people, elevating their self-esteem as well as helping you to be more influential. In my personal life, I found that showing appreciation brings me closer to my friends and colleagues.

To show appreciation, identify positive characteristics, then deliberately offer two types of comments—the first type remarks on the specific attribute you want to appreciate. The second calls out the same quality then connects the characteristic to a broader personality trait. Here are a few examples.

What you notice	**What you say**
You notice the other person regularly helps others after she completes her work.	"I appreciate how you are always willing to help others. You are a helpful person."
You notice the other person has a cheery disposition.	"I appreciate how you are always so upbeat. Having you around makes us all feel better."
You notice the other person can quickly create spreadsheets.	"I appreciate how quickly you can create a spreadsheet. You are very good at that."

When to use Direct and Indirect Speech

From my work, I found that expert performance leaders consistently build collaborative work teams. Having everyone involved creates an atmosphere in which the best ideas emerge. One of the leaders with whom I work had a straight style, frequently using commanding language to direct his reports. His people complained that they felt uninvolved and disconnected and that no one cared to hear their opinions.

I suggested he alter his language so that, rather than regularly offer commands, he should use inclusive statements, questions or suggestions that gain cooperation and promote teamwork. For example, rather than "The report must be done by 5 PM," say, "Let's all pitch in and get this done by 5."

Fischer and Orasanu, in a paper called *Cultural Diversity and Crew Communication* (presented at the Astronautical Congress in 1999), coined the term *mitigated speech* to describe aircraft crew interactions. Critical errors can occur if a crew fails to communicate directly with one another. The results of these communication failures have been tragic. In the business world, mitigated speech also has critical uses.

According to the authors, there are six levels of mitigation; each increases in deference and decreases and directness. I'll explain each, its appropriate use, and an example.

What	When to Use	Example
Level 1. Command - has no deference or indirect language	A command is particularly valuable when there is an urgent need to take action.	"Finish this report by 5 o'clock, or we will lose this customer."
Level 2. Team Obligation Statement – is inclusive of the whole team	When we want to create collaboration, we use a team obligation statement.	"Let's all work together to finish this report by 5 o'clock."
Level 3. Team Suggestion – uses a question to enhance inclusivity	Use the team suggestion to create inclusion while speaking in a less direct way.	"Why don't we all work together to see if we can finish this report by 5 o'clock?"
Level 4. Query – questioning used to be more indirect	One can use a question to prompt a group to think in a specific direction	"Do you think it would be helpful for us to get the report done by 5 o'clock?"
Level 5. Preference – a statement used indirectly to specify a bias	We use preference statements to guide the group down a particular path	"Perhaps we should look at different ways we can organize to get the report done."
Level 6. Hint – the most indirect form of mitigated speech	When you want to plant an idea without specifying the idea. Sometimes used to avoid conflict.	"I wonder if we have any important deadlines we should reach today."

By understanding your situations, you can maximize the different levels of mitigation. As mentioned above, when there is an urgent need to act, such as during an emergency, level one mitigation is most appropriate. When we wish to build highly connected and collaborative teams, higher levels of mitigation work more effectively. In situations that require extreme delicacy, mitigation at the highest levels proves valuable.

Openness

When we admit our mistakes, say we are sorry, or acknowledge when we need help, we exhibit openness and create a lasting connection and trust with others. Our ability to be open becomes one of our most critical influencing skills.

I had the opportunity to interview Tom Walter, who is by far one of the most vulnerable leaders I have met. In the early days at the company that he and his brothers started, Tasty Catering, Tom would use a direct and hierarchical command style which seemed to serve him well. As the business continued to mature, he believed all was running smoothly—that is, until two of his younger employees (who Tom and his brothers had identified as successors to run the company) confronted him. The two explained in no uncertain terms that if Tom and his brothers failed to change their command approach to running the organization, the two successors would leave.

He and his brothers were shocked. To their credit, rather than become defensive or resistant, they realized how valuable the feedback had been. They needed to change, to be more open, inclusive, and trusting of their employees, a change which led to a journey that continues to this day. Borrowing the ideas of premiere thought leaders, the brothers reshaped Tasty Catering into one of the most consistently profitable organizations in the country. Year over year, profit margins dependably outperform revenue growth. The company enjoys a remarkably high engagement score that reliably hovers in the 90th percentile. Of the over 5000 catering events last year, they refunded money on forty-four occasions only, less than one percent. Voluntary turnover is near nonexistent.

Tom embodies openness, freely discussing the mistakes he made during his youth. When Tom shares his rough early life with new hires, many of them having had tough beginnings, he fosters immediate connection and trust.

We do not have to have had such a difficult start to our lives as Tom did to be vulnerable. According to Patrick Lencioni, author of *The Five Dysfunctions of a Team*, Trust is the foundation of all great teamwork.

Situation	How Not to Be Open	How to Be Open
You forgot to complete a task for a friend at work.	I was so busy I couldn't get to your task.	I'm sorry. I completely forgot. It's my fault.
You can't create a spreadsheet that you need for a project.	It's not my fault. I was never trained to use spreadsheets this way.	I don't know how to create this spread-sheet. I need help.
You didn't make your quota for the month.	There were too many things out of my con-trol that prevented me from reaching quota.	Even though there were a lot of things out of my control, it's still my respon-sibility to reach quota. I should've asked for help.
Customers are complaining because of late orders.	I can't be held respon-sible if customers are calling to complain at 10 o'clock at night.	I totally missed this one. I need to check the logs to find out if customers are complaining late at night.
A beloved colleague is critically ill.	He will be okay. There's nothing to worry about.	This is very hard. I'm very concerned about our friend. I wish there were something I could do to make it better.

From the examples above, vulnerability takes courage, the courage to admit our concerns and insecurities. Many of us feel shame when remembering our least proud moments, yet it is the sharing of these moments that brings us closer. As Brene Brown, author and researcher, tells us, vulnerability is the birthplace of creativity and belonging. (Here is the link: https://www.youtube.com/watch?v=iCvmsMzlF7o .)

Deliberate Practice for Expert Performance

The ability to become highly influential requires practice.

- Choose one topic in this chapter and practice it for a week.
- If you don't know where to start, begin with honing your listening skills using reflective and empathic activities.
- Choose another topic each week to practice. You will be amazed that in a four-month timeframe, your ability to influence others will grow dramatically. You will undoubtedly notice a positive change in how people respond to you. I know because I've seen it in my clients and have done it myself!

Are you ready to master the power of influence? Assess yourself and understand your growth opportunities at www.expertperformance.com/power-of-influence.

CHAPTER 9

HOW TO GET TOP PERFORMANCE

Grow everyone to produce amazing outcomes just like your top producers

The Magic of Expert Performance

During an interview with a sales manager at a large pharmaceutical company, he confided that the loss of just one of his star salespeople would cost the company between four and five million dollars of lost revenue. Even more disconcerting, this staggering number fails to include follow on training and lost opportunity costs while the replacement ramps up to full capability. Having consulted to companies for over twenty years, our experience supports these extraordinary numbers. Our research found that Expert Performers contribute in the range of 50 percent more to 1200 percent more production than average employees. We found that the top 10 to 20 percent of employees in most companies produce a disproportionately large share of the revenue.

Because many organizations fail to grow expertise, numerous employees feel disenchanted and disengaged. Our research found that typical employees work at 75% capacity to as low as 25%. I can think of few business owners who would willingly hire someone knowing they would waste 75% of the paid compensation.

Understanding and transferring Expert Performance often means the difference between mediocre results and a fully engaged, productive workforce.

An Example

I had the opportunity to consult with a large credit card company who had a retail sales force. The organization wanted the sales staff to grow acceptance of their credit cards. The company asked me to investigate why some of their salespeople had achieved extraordinary results while others struggled.

We produced an Expert Performance Sales Success Map™

After identifying a group of top performers and a few average performers, we used our Expert Performance Success Map ™ processes to uncover the characteristics and behaviors of both groups. By contrasting the characteristics of these two groups, we were able to fully understand the expert performance characteristics that enabled experts to produce top results. These expert performance characteristics became the basis of an Expert Performance Sales Success Map™ to which we could compare all employees who were in the sales force.

We Applied the Expert Performance Sales Success Map™

Next, we identified a pilot group of 10 individuals who, together with their managers, completed a questionnaire based on the Expert Performance Sales Success Map™. During a feedback session with each participant and his or her manager, we identified areas of strength and challenges then created a development plan, including deliberate practice to augment strengths and address challenges.

Results

The results astounded us. After working on the development areas, the team increased overall sales performance by 38% in ninety days. Why was there such a dramatic improvement? Read on!

How to Become an Expert

In their groundbreaking article, *Expert Performance: Its Structure and Acquisition*, K. Anders Ericsson and Neil Charness explained how individuals become experts. To become an expert requires only two elements.

First, Practice, Practice

First, the individual must practice skills repeatedly and accurately. In their article, Ericsson and Charness observed that, on average, individuals must practice deliberately to reach expert level. For example, they found that symphony musicians who were highly accomplished but did not perform at the level of solo virtuoso had practiced 6000 to 7000 hours to arrive at their level of play. The authors found that the fewer the hours of practice, the less likely an individual would develop expertise.

In their summary, Ericsson and Charness write that anyone can become an expert in any field if (a big IF) the person has sufficient intelligence and practices long hours. Height may be the only limiter in some vocations, such as professional sports.

Simple, right? Like the old joke says, "How do you get to Carnegie Hall? - Practice, practice, practice."

Second, Get a Coach

The master coach exerts extraordinary influence on the development of expertise. Master coaches provide guidance that enables their students to practice precisely what is needed to create high performance.

Since I was in graduate school, I have studied opera singing with a master teacher, Dr. John Van Cura, whose students sing in houses across the world. He clears the pathway for these singers to become stars. One of his current students, for example, is an internationally known baritone who is making a career singing the role of Rigoletto.

No Coach Available – Use an Expert Performance Success Map™

At times, a master coach is not available, as was the case for the large credit card company example above. When a master coach is not available, the Expert Performance Success Map™ provides the direction of an expert coach, guiding the individual to practice precisely the behaviors, skills and capabilities that produce expertise.

If you want to become an expert leader, **complete the Expert Performance Leadership Success Assessment.** Email me at racioppo@expertperformance.com or call 847-840-9926, and I will set you up with the assessment.

Expert Performers Hold the Secrets to Solving Your Company Problems

When confronted with problems, organizations often use root-cause analysis to discover and address a problem's origin, and for most issues, the approach works well. Often, though, problems seem to defy root-cause analysis, particularly those that involve the complexity of human behavior.

When you encounter these complex issues, the expertise of your top people may hold the answers. Your company likely employs individuals who have resolved these complex challenges personally within their influence area. They may hold the key to a more comprehensive resolution.

Here's an example:

I recently had the opportunity to work with a moderately sized engineering consulting firm. We were asked to find out why part of the organization was losing first-and-second-year engineers. Attrition is a hugely complex issue and one ideally suited to using the wisdom of Expert Performers within an organization. The organization had examined root causes but remained unable to slow attrition. During our early conversations, we noticed that a group of individuals stayed past the two-year mark, and we became curious about what set those individuals apart from others. What was their expertise?

To understand that expertise, we produced an Expert Performance Success Map™ specifically to understand why some employees remained at the company. (I'll explain how to create one later in this chapter.) Although initially surprising, the results made sense.

We discovered two components contributed to retention. First, employees had personality attributes that enhanced self-advocacy and drive, easily enabling them to advance their careers more quickly than others. Second, the individuals who remained had an apprenticeship-style relationship with a coach or mentor. The coach taught the retained employee how to be successful at his work and within the whole organization.

These discoveries led us to create an Expert Performance Retention Success Map™ that is being used to both develop the younger employees and to raise the mentoring capabilities of the managers. Ultimately, the approach will increase retention and improve employee engagement.

Here's how you create an Expert Performance Success Map™

Step One - Identify Your Experts

Most leaders and organizations find identifying experts to be a relatively easy task. Let's say you have a problem with low sales. You have top performers whose sales regularly exceed expectations, and you wish to transfer that expertise to others in the organization. I've listed the selection criteria below.

Selection Criteria (use any combination of the items below)	**Sales Example**
Your experts will consistently produce at the top 10% of all employees over a 3 to 5 year.	You want to find those who are at the top 10% of sales.
Experts will be identified as top people by a group of leaders.	Ask your leaders who they think their top people are. Rather than look at sales only, use other criteria such as attitude and drive.
Experts have influence and made a positive impact beyond their departments.	Look for salespeople who have led committees, mentored others, or have innovated across the company.
Peers and others recognize these people as leaders.	Find those individuals who are mentioned by others as leaders and top performers.

Our experience tells us that you need 3 – 5 experts to produce a comprehensive expert model. Sometimes we find the need to select more people so that the experts represent multiple departments. You may also wish to choose several non-experts (optional) to contrast expert and non-expert performance.

Note: If you cannot identify individuals who have all the expert performance characteristics you need, build a map that combines the attributes of more than one.

Step Two - Create an Expert Performance Success Map™

One of our clients asked us to discover the expert performance characteristics of top superintendents who routinely outperformed others in the organization. A construction superintendent has a significant impact on the success or failure of a project, so understanding the expertise of the very best made financial sense. Using the expert performance mapping process, we created an Expert Performance Superintendent Success Map™ of high performing superintendents.

Below, you will find the questions we ask to produce an Expert Performance Success Map™. You may want to record the interviews for later review.

Questions to ask to produce the Expert Performance Success Map™	Example Expert Performance Superintendent Success Map™ of a field superintendent at an example company – leads electrical construction projects
1. Beliefs and Motivations: What is important to you personally in your work? (This is a motivation and beliefs question that taps into a person's primary beliefs. Usually, individuals will have no more than 4 to 6 responses.)	1. (Coaches and Mentors Others) I find it important to move each person through a process from one area of expertise to another as each skill is mastered. 2. (Communicates effectively) It's important to communicate well with the team, vendors, and contractors. No misunderstandings. I handle conflicts before they can become destructive. 3. (Financial Acumen) Superintendents must understand the financials of a project. 4. (Lead) I believe in the importance of clear outcomes, which we should achieve through people who we have grown and developed.

2. Evidence: Thinking about how you answered question one, how do you know you have each one of the items? (This question asks for evidence. What do we notice when we have successfully implemented our motivations and beliefs?)	1. Everyone has a one-on-one development relationship with a leader or supervisor. 2. I notice few misunderstandings. We address conflict quickly and without blow-ups 3. Through the superintendent, everyone understands where projects are financially. 4. Goals and outcomes have been clearly stated. Everyone knows what these goals are and are working toward them.
3. Strategies: Again thinking about how you answered question one, let's walk through each item and understand the strategies you use to fulfill your beliefs and motivations. (By tapping into strategies, we fully understand how an individual achieves the results they want.)	Because strategies may have considerable detail, I have shown a sample below in a separate table. Each strategy corresponds to a belief or motivation mentioned in step 1 above.

Below are sample strategies for the same Expert Performance Superintendent Success Map™ interview above. Because of length, I did not include all strategies that came from the map.

1. Coaches and Mentors

I have weekly conversations with each employee to help them grow and develop.
I give regular feedback to my people almost daily to help them overcome problems and get better at their work.
I assign progressively more difficult projects to each employee so that they can grow and develop.
I show by example what it takes to produce good work.
I have a plan in mind for each person to grow and develop them.
I continually think of ways to prepare my people so I can help promote my employees to higher levels in the organization.
I become the learner in a mentoring situation so that I can understand the person I am mentoring.

2. Effectively Communicates

When I influence, I make sure that I understand the other person's motivations.

I take time to listen so that I fully understand what the person is saying.

I have regular meetings between the field and general contractors to be assured that we are all communicating clearly with one another.

I address conflict head-on and make sure that it doesn't get hurtful.

If I have a conflict with a general contractor, I call a meeting to address it as soon as possible.

I hold regular meetings with the team so that everybody understands not only the status of the project but what is happening in the organization as a whole.

3. Financial Acumen

I know where my projects are almost daily financially—at least weekly.

I take courses at my company to understand the financials of the company.

I teach others how to manage the finances of a project.

I stay on top of billings, making sure that they are put out timely and paid.

I make everyone financially responsible for their part of the project.

4. Lead

I share expectations upfront so the team can achieve.

Goals are team goals and are communicated that way.

"Meets" is unacceptable–I help the team strategize for "Exceeds" level.

I promote competition, comparing results with other teams.

I gather and use performance measurements.

I make sure everyone feels empowered to solve problems.

I allow people to make mistakes as long as they don't put the project significantly in danger.

I make sure people feel that they have responsibility for the job and feel connected to it.

Step Three – Create the final Expert Performance Superintendent Success Map™

From the above sets of motivation, beliefs, evidence, and strategies, we create an Expert Performance Superintendent Success Map™ to coach and develop the superintendents. We try to use fewer than thirty questions, since exceeding that number causes rater fatigue.

If we have too many questions, we use two methods to reduce the number. The first way asks experts which questions they think are valuable. For this example, we asked the senior leaders to rate the importance of the items to the person's position. We then eliminated low-rated items.

The second method involves giving the Expert Performance Success Map™ to an entire group with whom we are working then statistically analyze which items correlate with an individual's success. Although this process provides more accurate information, timing and resources often stand in the way of using this method. However, if we were using the Expert Performance Success Map™ as a performance evaluation tool, we want to run analytics to assure that the map complies with labor laws. Since in the example we were using the map as a development aid only, running such an analysis was unnecessary.

Below you will find an example superintendent Expert Performance Success Map™ Benchmark. The map is given to, in this case, superintendents so that we might grow their expertise.

Since each item is a behavior, we can rate each item as to how often the person exhibits that behavior. I usually use the following scale to rate each item:

Almost Always

Frequently

Usually

Seldom

Almost Never

Superintendent Expert Performance Success Map™ Benchmark

Coaches and Mentors	Creates a work environment that maximizes people's growth and development.
	Helps the team grow the skills necessary to produce project outcomes.
	Provides promotion opportunities.
	Demonstrates an example of hard work.
Effectively Communicates	When influencing, connects desired outcomes to the other person's motivation.
	Listens well.
	Works to create open communication between operations, field, vendors, GC's, and owners to assure efficiency and profitability.
	Continuously communicates with the team through activities such as daily meetings.
	Brings up issues even at the risk of conflict or discomfort.
Manages Finances	Runs a financially successful project, including budgets and margins.
	Monitors how money is being spent in the project, assuring a profitable outcome.
	Understands how to read financial reports for a project.
	Manages billings effectively.
Leads Effectively	Holds everyone to high standards of performance.
	Gives freedom to people to make decisions while functioning on their own.
	Is not punitive when individuals make mistakes.
	Encourages employees to take responsibility for major portions of a project.
	Helps employees to feel empowered to solve their own problems, not accepting excuses.
	Helps individuals feel connected to and responsible for the job.

Step Four – Apply the Expert Performance Success Map™ Benchmark

Once we have created the final Expert Performance Success Map™, we can use the map as a 360 instrument to rate the individual. We recommend conducting the 360s every eighteen months, beginning six months after the person joins the firm. A 360, in case you're unfamiliar with the term, provides feedback from multiple perspectives. The employee rates himself. The manager, peers, and direct reports, if any, rate the employee.

Step Five – Coach, Develop, and Mentor

Once you have finished the Expert Performance Success Map™, you will want everyone in your organization who you wish to develop to complete the Expert Performance Success Map™. Here are the steps:

1. After each person fills out the Expert Performance Success Map™, which compares everyone to the highest performers, create a development plan. From the example above, the superintendent, the manager, and a representative from our company reviewed each item flagging both strengths and challenges.

2. Have an experienced coach (I do this for my organization) meet with the employee and the employee's manager to discuss the results of the 360 feedback. Here are the steps.

    - Discuss the person's future, asking questions such as: "Where would you like to be in your career in five years? If you could add anything to your job today, what would it be? What are you most proud of in your work?"

    - Looking at each item, flag those showing high strength and those that present challenges. We want to focus on maximizing strengths since the individual will often address challenges as the person pursues his or her future goals.

    - From the flagged items, choose no more than six that the individual would like to address. Ensure that the person represents his or her strengths in the selected items.

    - Towards the end of the coaching session, ask the individual if he or she agrees that addressing the items will help the person to reach his or her desired future. If the answer is no, swap out items with those that meet the individual's needs.

- Create a list of goals from the flagged items. Goals should be specific and time-bound.

3. Review the development goals monthly to determine progress. Without frequent development conversation, your younger employees will leave within the first year or two.

4. Every eighteen months, again administer the Expert Performance Success Map™ followed by step 2.

Results You Should Expect

I worked with an electrical contractor who suffered from a lack of project managers who had had enough experience to lead others and manage significant portions of major projects. There were just not enough performers to run a challenging and complicated project.

I was meeting with one of the newer project managers, Tom, who was about to take on a significant role in a new project to help the city of Chicago—rebuild a transit line. Even though Tom sat in the lower end of the company's bench, leadership saw promise in him. I had created an Expert Performance Project Manager Success Map™ for the organization's project managers based on the expertise of their senior leaders, and I was there to review Tom's feedback.

I'll never forget the comment Tom made after we walked through the results and created his development plan. "I guess I will have to start managing people." The organization thrust Tom, who had never managed anyone, into a highly visible, critical project. With our coaching help and the mentoring of others, Tom and the project succeeded. Tom remained with the company, led even more people, and a few years later the company promoted him to vice president.

We continued to help others in the organization to grow and develop using the Expert Performance Project Manager Success Map ™. As a result of using the map, the organization filled their bench strength, completed additional complex projects, and increased revenue from approximately $90 million to well over $600 million in less than ten years.

Technology

New and improved technology from companies such as SkillNet (www.skillnet.com) easily enables organizations to conduct 360's, do coaching, and enjoy frequent growth conversations using only a smartphone.

Deliberate Practice for Expert Performance

If you wish to create high performance in an area of your business or transfer expertise from those who are extraordinary producers, you want to use the Expert Performance Success Map™.

If you want to understand your own Leadership Expertise, use this link to take the free version of Expert Performance Leadership Success™ (insert LINK)

- Identify areas in which you wish to increase expertise.
- Conduct the interview shown in this chapter.
- Produce an Expert Performance Success Map™ benchmark based on the expertise.
- Measure people against the benchmark. (New technologies allow us to repeat the benchmarks more frequently. We recommend at least once a year.)
- Provide feedback and create a development plan for each person.
- Continue to grow and develop your people. Development creates a great relationship between you and your employees. You will want to have development conversations at least monthly.

Are you ready to get top performance? Assess yourself and understand your growth opportunities at

www.expertperformance.com/get-top-performance.

CHAPTER 10

BUILD AN EXPERT PERFORMANCE TEAM

Build your team to produce extraordinary results

From my research and experience, I have found that top-performing organizations are much more likely to have top-notch, A-level team members (expert performers) at the top of the organization. Expert Performing leaders recognize several essential truths:

- No single leader can know everything. Team members will compensate for the challenges of the leader and other team members.

  Team members will have talents that fall into one or more of these domains: execution, strategic thinking, relationship buiding, and influencing. Top leaders take advantage of each strength domain to speed the progress of the team.

- No individual leader can do it all. Top leaders must surround themselves with experts to whom they can delegate work, trusting that the efforts will be of high quality. (Without the ability to delegate, the leaders must do the tasks themselves and will become a bottleneck, slowing the whole company.)

  One of my clients, who leads a team, finds difficulty delegating to team members, fearing that they will not produce results at the same level he does. He explained that they make mistakes that he must catch. By helping him raise the capability of his people, he no longer needs to be wary of assigning tasks.

- The team together creates better outcomes and is generally smarter than the sum of its parts. A team comprised of people who have different expertise assures high-performance results for the organization

Because each team member sees issues from a different point of view, team members will combine their expertise to produce better ideas and solutions.

Conversely, companies that struggle often have one or more team members whose weaknesses impede the progress of the organization and cause the leader and other team members to compensate for the weak person's lowered performance. One of my clients hired a department manager who, although competent within his group, had a significant challenge; he had little inclination to work with the rest of the leadership team. Even though coaching helped, progress remained slow. I advised my client that, since the organization was suffering financially because of this individual, the leader may not have time to develop the manager. The leader replaced the manager with a much more cooperative individual. Not surprisingly, performance increased rapidly throughout the team and company.

The Six Critical Steps for Building a High Performance Team

From our research, we discovered these six critical steps for building an expert performance team:

1. Focus on positivity and the future.
2. Build openness and trust.
3. Foster amazing decision-making.
4. Make decisions stick.
5. Hold each other responsible.
6. Focus on outcomes.

Focus on Positivity and the Future

Unlike most leaders who focus solely on business outcomes, top-performing executives first emphasize the commitment of their people to common purpose and goals, knowing that achievement will follow. Their actions and communications set an example of positivity while creating a compelling vision of the future. They continually redefine past errors and mistakes as opportunities to learn how to produce extraordinary future results.

Here are examples of two different ways to achieve results, one traditional and one used by experts.

Traditional Leadership	Positive and Future Expert Leadership
It's crucial that we hit our goals for this year so that we may have enough cash flow to run our operations. We made a lot of mistakes over the last six months, and we can't afford to repeat these.	I am feeling so confident that we will reach our goals this year, helping us to make our organization stronger and providing more rewards to you as a company associate. Over the last year, we hit a few speed bumps, and I know we have learned much that will be valuable for reaching our goals.

Leading people's thinking into the future grows creativity and passion. As a team leader, your job is to help individuals to see, feel, and hear the future vividly.

Build Openness and Trust

One of my clients, who works in the IT outsourcing business, asked me to help with a difficult challenge. The IT outsourcing company's (I'll call it XYZ), becomes the IT provider for its customers. Each time my client's company secures a new contract, many of the contracting company's employees become employees of the XYZ business. Because the two organizations have different cultures and approaches to their work, the differences can lower performance and erode the relationship between XYZ and the client.

Usually, two camps develop, one from the XYZ company and another from the client. In one such situation, the XYZ company asked me to help them form a single team with a particularly well-known, high-profile client. As we began to work through initial exercises and conversations, the activities exposed one of the two organization's biggest challenges. Each team believed that the other was deliberately withholding information, thereby contributing to slowdowns and poor performance.

An inability to form relationship and trust remains prevalent in most organizations. Most of us fear that admitting weaknesses and difficulties diminishes us in the eyes of others. Since the first task for any group is to form relationships and connections, I began with exercises and tools such as DiSC and a team assessment from Wiley Publishing (Please contact me directly at 847-840-9926 or email me at racioppo@expertperformance.com, and I will point you in the right direction to find the best team tools for you to use.) These helped team members feel sufficient trust so that they felt comfortable discussing their challenges openly.

Teams repeatedly leave me surprised, often exceeding my expectations through their courage and resilience. The XYZ and client group offered one such instance. After several exercises to build more relationship and trust, one of the members of the client group spoke without prompting. "Just because we don't give you information (to the XYZ group) doesn't mean we actually have it." This brief declaration broke a deadlock that had slowed the growth of the two teams from the beginning and opened a critical dialogue for cooperation and progress. After this valuable comment, the two teams unified their focus away from mistrust towards the important outcomes required by the client company.

For those who work in teams, the next step to success starts with our ability to connect, then to have the courage to challenge and admit our concerns. The example above illustrates the power of connectedness and trust, which opened the door to growth. Here are a few suggestions to use to foster openness and trust:

Steps	Examples
1. Focus on the need for two groups as one team pursuing the same results.	"Your team serves a higher purpose both to one another and to the entire organization. If your team were wildly successful, what goals would your team reach? What would be your role?"
2. Offer exercises and activities that allow individuals to open up.	"Sometimes working on a team can be challenging. Think about your team in the future. If the future were marvelous, what would change? What would you change personally?" Here's another excellent question. "What has been the most challenging time in your work career, and how did you overcome it?"

Foster Amazing Decision Making

Most organizations face a challenge with decision-making, particularly the ability to explore every aspect of an idea. Most people avoid conflict, fearing that such conflict will lead to hurt feelings or momentum loss. Such avoidance can be catastrophic. For example, in 1986, NASA lost the lives of seven Challenger astronauts because of defective O-Rings which, compromised by cold weather, failed, leading to explosive gas leakage and devasting engine failure. President Ronald Regan formed the Rogers Commission to investigate the accident and found that NASA's culture and decision-making process had been key contributing factors. NASA engineers had disregarded warnings about the dangers posed by Morton-Thiokol's poor O-ring design.

Instead of a deep dive into the risks of a cold-weather launch, the NASA team, by deciding to move forward despite contrary evidence, set in motion the worst space program disaster in history.

Your organization must pursue every nuance of a decision, engaging all team members to participate fully and freely without fear of hurt feelings or slowing momentum. Without an in-depth inspection, decision making suffers. Why is this deep inspection necessary? Here is one example from the work of Daniel Kahneman and Amos Tversky, who uncovered the irrationality of most decision making.

Researchers chose two groups. The first group received this problem:

> Imagine that the US is preparing for the outbreak of a rare contagious disease, which is expected to kill 600 people. Medical personnel proposed two programs, and you are to choose either A or B.
>
> **Problem 1**
>
> Program A: 200 people will be saved.
>
> Program B:
>
> 1/3 probability that 600 people will be saved
>
> a 2/3 probability that no people will be saved.
>
> Which of the two programs would you favor?

Results – An overwhelming majority chose Program A, to save 200 lives (note that 400 people will not be saved).

Problem 2: A second group received the same setup but with a choice between two other programs, C and D. Which would you choose?

Program C – 400 people will die.

Program D

There is a 1/3 chance that **nobody** will die.

There is 2/3 chance that 600 people will die.

Results – For Problem 2, the overwhelming majority selected Program D.

Explanation

Here is the fascinating thing – the two problems are ***identical***. The only difference between the two is in the wording. Let me explain.

- In Problem 1, researchers framed the problem as a **gain** – the subjects chose Program A to save 200 people for sure, even though 400 would die.

- In Problem 2, Program C (the same outcome as Program A) was framed as a **loss**–400 people will die. Still, 200 people will live–precisely like Program A, just written differently.

  Program D and Program B results are identical, just worded differently.

Here is the moral of the story. People will choose gain over loss, a choice that is not scientifically or logically based.

The explanation above is one example of the tendency for people to make decisions that are not factually or mathematically sound. Such decision-making can result in organizational challenges.

Here are several steps to ensure better decision-making.

Steps for Better Decision-Making
Assure that everyone is heard. By deliberately calling on every team member, even those who are introverted and may not speak out, we assure ourselves of having wide-ranging input. Ask where each person stands on the pending decision.
Encourage your team to dig deep into each person's thinking, exploring every corner of an idea.
When exploring an idea, use math calculations as often as possible, when applicable. For example, many marketing and sales decisions hide hidden costs that reduce profitability.

Make Decisions Stick!

Returning to the XYZ company in the previous example, the team listed goals and steps that would enable achievement of their results. Everyone in the group offered ideas, some were adopted, and others not. The group decided which ideas would form their plan to go forward. Several months after my work with the team, the group continued to deliver successful results. The fracturing between the two groups had disappeared, and the XYZ and client participants continue to act as one successful organization.

After a team makes decisions, everyone must be on board and feel an obligation to comply with the choices. What makes this possible? Here are a few steps to consider to make decisions stick.

Steps to Make Decisions Stick
As in the previous step, be sure that everyone participates in an opportunity to express themselves.
Make the decision clear and precise. Explain what you all agree to do and by when. Use precision language, i.e., the language of the senses. What will you notice when you have committed to the decision? What will you hear, feel, see, touch, taste, or smell?
Ask every person in the group if they have any concerns about the decision that was just made. Again, every person wants to be heard.

Hold Each Other Responsible

I was working with the XYZ team, and I noticed that several distracting behaviors occurred during meetings. Participants often glanced at their phones and computers to answer texts and emails. Some of the individuals left the room. When members of a team feel distractions, they often fail to give entirely, shortchanging their contributions.

I pointed out the situation in a neutral manner. "I can't help notice that some of you are answering texts and emails. Others have had to leave the room. We miss your participation in the group. Are these behaviors okay for everyone?" Incidentally, the leader of the group was one of the most frequent violators.

Interestingly, most members of the team felt that these distractions slowed progress and should be avoided.

Because the group no longer worried about hurt feelings, they could actively engage in problem-solving to address even the extenuating circumstances. One of the members of the team told the group that he had to take phone calls and emails because he was responding to emergencies. The group asked, "Can someone else handle emergencies while you're in meetings for an hour or two?" He thought for a moment, then replied, "That would be possible. I need to ask one of the other team members to take my calls. My temporary replacement can brief me later."

The group leader admitted that by answering emails and texts, he was one of the biggest offenders. When the rest of the team found his behavior distracting, he acknowledged that he could wait until breaks to review correspondence. He made a reasonable request of the group, asking if breaks could be slightly more frequent.

As a result of the discussion, the group agreed to limit computer and phone use to emergencies, delegating others on their team to watch for important information and to hold each other accountable for the new behavior.

How often has your team interrupted productive conversations with glances at emails and text messages?

Holding each other responsible for group actions and norms is one of the most influential behaviors a team can employ. Such new measures can reduce irritation and dramatically increase productivity.

How to hold each other responsible
With the group, define acceptable behaviors such as arriving on time for meetings, completing assignments for the group, avoiding the use of electronics, etc.
The leader must make a public commitment to the desired behaviors.
As the leader, you must hold people responsible for the desired behaviors; otherwise, no one will. Other members of the team will assume the behaviors are ok.
Periodically review behaviors that the team finds helpful and those they find distracting.

Focus on Outcomes

When the XYZ company engaged with FinanceCo (not the company's name), two seemingly dissimilar outcomes become apparent. Since XYZ was bonused based on efficiencies and cost reduction, the XYZ company worked to reduce FinanceCo's profit-consuming activities. Members of the client company wanted to continue to contribute while preserving their jobs. When XYZ took over the IT services, FinanceCo team members felt marginalized, threatened, and in jeopardy. Although job reductions initially occurred with the engagement of the XYZ company, FinanceCo had planned no further layoffs.

In summary, the two organizations appeared headed in different directions.

1. The XYZ company outcomes included cost reductions and improved efficiencies, leading to better financial performance for FinanceCo.

2. The FinanceCo employees wanted to preserve jobs and to assert their positions of influence and contribution.

The XYZ company with its efforts on management by numbers made numerous requests for information data from FinanceCO while ignoring the stress they created. With preservation and status top of mind, FinanceCO team members unconsciously thwarted the XYZ company's efforts, responding slowly to XYZ's information requests.

I intervened to help the teams focus on the same results. The steps are listed below.

Steps	Example
1. Help team members realize the concerns that their fellow associates might have.	I worked with both teams to understand the positions of both the XYZ company and FinanceCo team members. Once fully exposed, the outcome for each group seemed reasonable to the other group.
2. Emphasize and focus on a broader and more encompassing outcome that creates a win-win for all parties. Enable team participants to understand that they could advance themselves while ensuring that their colleagues reach their desired results.	I helped the teams realize they had a common desire to help FinanceCo IT customers to be more successful. Doing so would also ensure job stability, contribution, and improved efficiencies.
3. Cement in place the idea that multiple groups are one team.	Working with both groups, we established the idea that we were one team, an idea that helped the team to see both groups as one instead of multiple identities.

Deliberate Practice for Expert Performance

Expert performing leaders produce top teams. Without these top-notch groups, leaders find themselves distracted, doing the job of their subordinates while neglecting more important matters. Follow the six steps below that will help you to create the high performing teams that you need. I provided an exercise for each step.

1. Focus on positivity and the future.

   Each time you hear a challenge or a problem, ask, "What should we do instead?" Asking this question focuses the team on the future.

2. Build openness and trust.

   By regularly asking what your people need, you help them become more vulnerable and trusting.

3. Foster amazing decision-making.

   Involve each team member in discussions, asking for pros and cons. This action will encourage everyone to participate and to engage in healthy conversation.

4. Make decisions stick.

   Each time the team makes a decision, ask every member to agree. If, for example, some members struggle with the decision, you have an excellent opportunity to find out why and then gain commitment.

5. Hold each other responsible.

   Be sure that you enforce agreements between members. Once you set an example, others will begin to hold each other responsible.

6. Focus on outcomes.

   Assure that everyone focuses on agreed-to results for the team. There is no time for personal or hidden agendas.

Are you ready to build an expert team? Assess yourself and understand your growth opportunities at

www.expertperformance.com/build-an-expert-team.

CHAPTER 11

FIND THE BRIGHT SHINING STARS

Foster an organization to bring out the brilliance in your people

When I worked at IBM, I had the opportunity to hire college students to sell IBM personal computers to their peers. One of these potential college reps, Rick, applied for a position. Looking over his resume and recalling his interview, I felt uncertain whether Rick would succeed in the job. He presented as shy and willing to step into the shadows. I felt torn, so rather than make a decision, I placed his resume on my back burner and continued to interview others. Rick was not going to go away quickly. Through persistent calling and inquiries, he wore me down. The calls went on for a while, so I finally agreed to add him to our student sales staff. I figured that anyone so determined might have a reasonable chance of success as a salesperson.

After a few weeks, Rick asked to talk. He explained that he felt uncomfortable, pushy, and awkward when urging his fellow students to purchase an IBM personal computer. I listened, paused a moment then said, "Think about a time when you did not make a relatively expensive purchase but wanted to very badly. Perhaps you even had the money. How did you feel?"

Even before he spoke, I could see a look of regret register on his face. "Yes, I wished I had made that purchase. I just felt as though I shouldn't. It was too much money."

I explained, "Many times, people want to make an important purchase, so when you talk to customers about the reasons they want to buy and what the purchase will do for them, you give them permission to do something important–for themselves."

Rick thought for a moment then flashed an aha look of comprehension. Over the next year, his weekly sales grew until IBM recognized him as one of the top student reps in the nation.

I'll never forget the experience of initial doubts about Rick and how he turned himself into a top performer. In my career as a coach and consultant, I have witnessed Rick stories endlessly repeated, and from these situations learned valuable lessons. Never doubt the importance of our role as leaders to help our employees discover the powers within to turn themselves into bright shining stars.

Five ways to find the bright shining stars:

My work with leadership and my interviews with top people have helped me to identify the five most important ways to find the bright shining stars within each person. Like a good gardener, we as leaders provide the conditions which turn the seemingly mundane into the exceptional.

1. Understand a person's strengths and have them work on these every day.

   One of my clients, Paul, runs a division of his larger organization. He performs exceptionally well, delivering the highest revenue and largest profit in his part of the company. Recently, one of Paul's largest customers complained that he and his team were often late delivering project results. Closer to home, several of Paul's employees expressed concern that Paul made decisions without input, rarely explaining his reasoning, causing them to feel undervalued and left out, that their opinions did not count. As the department has grown, Paul has also recognized, as did his leadership, that he needs to develop more leaders beneath him so that he could delegate work and build his part of the company.

   As a consultant, and well before the client does, I frequently notice the strengths (the bright shining star within) that are often hidden and unknown to others and the client. To help in the identification of these hidden elements, I usually offer assessments, since these take the emotion out of feedback and provide objective information beyond my observations, helping the unknown become known.

   Paul uses terrific strengths–an ability to think through ideas thoroughly, create stability, comprehend and remember details, and foster teamwork. Sometimes though, a person's strengths clash with the organizations' culture. Paul's organization, like many companies, favors leaders who make decisions quickly and drive their people for results, both of which do not mirror Paul's assets.

We decided to emphasize Paul's strengths, teaching him how to lead through his most exceptional talents. Because Paul had a knack for bringing people together, we decided to teach Paul how to manage collaboratively instead of using a top-down approach.

As a note, top-down approaches that drive for results become essential in situations which require quick decision-making to address an urgent condition. For example, a company may be losing money or market share and need strong leadership to "right the ship." At Paul's organization, no such emergencies existed. Immediate action was not required. Instead, collaboration, engagement, and cooperation among all employees would address the situation with the complaining customer and unhappy employees.

During a brainstorming session, Paul convened his team, which identified the ideal connection with the troubled customer. They then listed tasks to create an optimal relationship. Paul facilitated the group, helping members focus on three or four tasks that would provide an immediate client benefit. He assigned the tasks to small groups who later reported back on their progress.

This intervention with Paul worked at two levels. First, his team directly addressed a deteriorating customer situation. Second, and more importantly, Paul used a collaborative and facilitative management style, which more suited his strengths as well as allowed his team to participate in decision-making and the operation of the group. Doing so helped foster more opportunities in Paul's department, allowing Paul to recognize those who had leadership capabilities.

By focusing Paul on his talents instead of trying to make him into the image of other members of the organization, Paul resolved a customer problem while growing his team and its newest leaders. Paul found a bright shining star within himself and others.

2. Know what patterns make a person successful.

Max works for a boutique engineering firm employing eight people. Liz, the owner, talked to me of her concern that Max was not producing enough revenue to meet his performance goals. He has struggled with a new software program that calculates forces and stress points, preferring to use spreadsheets developed at previous jobs. Unfortunately, these old tools further slowed his work, causing him to fall further behind. Assessments show that Max does not fit the position well, and perhaps the company should not have hired him.

We all want to avoid a bad fit to avoid bringing on ill-suited people into our organization. On occasion, we, like Liz, make wrong hiring choices. Because of Liz's good nature, she wanted to find a way to help Max succeed. "He's been with us two years already, and I think it unfair to terminate him without giving him the chance to succeed," Liz told me. "See what you can do."

Max began to lose hope that he could succeed in his current position. He had been successful in previous jobs and wondered why he could not keep up in Liz's company.

The answer became apparent. Using our proprietary tool called the Expert Performance Success Map™, I uncovered the patterns that Max used to achieve success at his previous jobs. (There's a full explanation of how to produce and Expert Performance Success Map™ in the chapter "How to Get Top Performance.") In the table below, I show his success pattern (left column) from a previous successful position next to an explanation (right column) of why Max cannot use the past success pattern in his current job.

Expert Performance Success Map™	**Current Position**
Works with a sales team who identify prospects, then he can secure contracts with "warm" prospects.	He has no sales team. He has to identify prospects independently. He does not know methods to find new clients.
Able to secure contracts with identified prospects.	Can sell a contract only if the prospect is a warm lead.
Had a colleague to perform calculations which helped Max to stay caught up. Max would then check the computations.	He has to do his calculations manually and does not know the new software. Without help, Max falls behind on revenue production.
Max would delegate some of the project-management activities to an intern or direct report.	Max has no direct reports or interns and must perform all project management.

As you can see from the table above, significant elements of the Expert Performance Success Map™ (left column) are absent from the current position (right column). As we walked through Max's Expert Performance Success Map™, Max felt relief, realizing how the missing elements from his current job slowed his performance. He understood that success in Liz's company required additional resources, resources that he did not have.

I explained the situation to Liz, suggesting the following. "First, teach Max how to sell. He can close a warm lead, so we need to help him find those leads. Second, bring Max up to speed on the new software even though, given his assessment scores, Max will feel challenged. I also recommend that we set performance goals for Max so that Max understands his performance targets."

Liz thought for a moment then replied, "So the next step is to put together goals and hope Max can learn how to sell and use the new software?"

I nodded.

Liz shook her head and then spoke, "I hope he can do this. I want to keep him, but if it means adding resources which I can't afford–well, I don't know."

"Yes, you have a tough decision to make," I acknowledged.

During a follow-up call with Liz several weeks later, I expected her to tell me that Max was still struggling, but her observation surprised me. Because Max learned that his current situation was not due to lack of ability, he felt empowered. Max had dug into the software system to learn how to use it and began to make substantive progress. By creating a clear list of specific goals for the team, Liz helped to set expectations and outcomes, further improving attitude. Finally, Liz scheduled a team meeting that identified ways to increase sales.

By understanding Max's Expert Performance Success Map™, we were able to improve Max's attitude, create empowerment, and move the entire organization forward.

When you understand, as a leader, the patterns that make people successful, you create a powerful competitive advantage for your organization. An Expert Performance Success Map™ shines a bright light on the shining star within.

3. Offer respect for what your people do.

   Colonel Jill Morgenthaler started her career as an ROTC graduate commissioned as a second lieutenant in the United States Army. Upon retirement, she had reached the rank of full colonel, certainly an achievement for any person, and even more difficult for a woman in a then-mostly-man's world. I asked her what was most important to her as a leader.

   Colonel Jill told me:

   "I think that one of the most important things is–it's all about respect. And as a leader [...] you can show it by taking an interest in who your people are. You can show it by working side by side as they do their job. You'll never do it as well. But when you give, when you try to do their job, you have a better appreciation of what they do. And with that appreciation comes your respect, and that respect will come back to you when people realize that you understand what they do, how hard it is, that you can't do it as well. [...], that's vulnerable. And yet, that's what brings respect into the workplace."

   She told me the story of seeing several subordinates who were changing a tire on a large truck. Wanting to understand their job, she stopped to ask if they would teach her how to change the tire. One of the soldiers replied, "Ma'am, you don't want to do this. It's heavy, and you'll get your uniform dirty." She reaffirmed that she wanted to learn. After instruction and hard work, she and her subordinates changed the tire. She told them, "This is really hard work that you guys do. Thank you." As she walked away, she saw big grins on those soldiers' faces. They knew she appreciated and understood. Above all, she had respect for them.

   Tom Walter of Tasty Catering is the Chief Cultural Officer for an exceptional organization. When most organizations consider a 70% or above engagement to be stellar, Tasty Catering routinely scores in the 90+ percentile. People feel connected to the business and expend sincere effort to make the company work well. As a result, each year profits grow *faster* than revenue, a notable feat for any organization. Tom talks about respect:

   "[...] first we have to earn respect and respect is not [...] controlled by me. It's controlled by [the other person who decides when he or she respects Tom. Tom doesn't say, "You have to respect me."] So I have to earn the respect."

By showing respect and understanding an employee's job, you do the following:

- Your employees give you insight into how they fulfill themselves and what they do exceptionally well.
- You have the opportunity to assign to your employees more of the tasks that create fulfillment.
- You create more engagement.
- You grow your organization.
- Above all, you help each person find the bright shining star within.

4. Build a compelling culture in which everyone can shine.

I had the opportunity to interview Joe Damico, who was a founder of a private equity firm, The RoundTable Healthcare Management group in Lake Forest, Illinois. Jim had been COO at Allegiance Healthcare, which had employed over 20,000 people.

> "The thing that is important to me personally as a leader would be probably, as a generalization, would be culture[...]. You spend more time of your waking moments with the people you work with than your family and anything else. [...] It's how you treat people, how you act over the course of an extended period of time. You also want to surround yourself with people that want to treat everybody, as simple as it sounds, the way that they wanted to be treated. I've never met anybody that doesn't want to be treated well. I've never been anybody that doesn't want to be mentioned by their name."

Austin Werner, who started a company called The Real Seal in Schaumburg, Illinois, is an up-and-comer. With his five star rating on Yelp and his exemplary culture, Austin has a clear sightline for success. Most companies struggle to fill their organization with engaged people, but Austin's people spoke with enthusiasm and appreciation for their chance to be employed by Austin's company.

When I asked him where he wanted to take his company, he answered as most people would expect, mentioning growth, size, and added locations for his business. When pressed though, he said what he *truly* wanted to do was, "**Make my company a great place to work**."

Mark Crea, the executive director of Feed My Starving Children, understands the value of purpose in culture. In world locations where starvation is frequent, parents feed their children hardened lumps of clay to fill their stomachs and reduce hunger feelings. Without proper nutrition, many die. Mark and his team make an enormous difference. Since its inception, the organization's employees and its 1.3 million volunteers have provided 2.3 billion nutritious meals, feeding hungry children around the world and saving thousands from starvation, all of this with a budget of only $81 million.

Mark told me that the purpose of his company was twofold: to change the lives of malnourished children and to provide volunteers with a life-giving experience of volunteering.

If you get the culture right, success follows.

One of my clients produces manufactured metal products. At my first visit to the organization's main office, I immediately felt uncomfortable. Employees did not greet me or glance up from their work. The office was quiet, too quiet—no laughter or interaction. When I joined meetings, management filled these with accusations regarding mistakes and errors. Morale hit a low point.

Working with the plant, we began massive culture change, moving from negativity to high positive regard. I taught leaders how to focus on the future rather than the mistakes of the past. We changed conversations to ones of encouragement, talking to employees about what leaders wanted, not what they did not want.

In most client engagements, customers have breakthrough moments, and this project was no exception. During a training about encouragement and positivity, the plant manager interrupted the class, surprising the group by telling them that no one was to yell at anyone, anymore—no more raising of voices. There was a moment of quiet hesitation as people looked at one another. As one of the biggest offenders, the plant manager had instantly affirmed a significant culture shift.

Today, both the plant team and the central office have created a terrific culture that supports loyalty and high performance.

When the culture is right, the bright shining stars within each person emerge, bringing out the best in everyone.

5. Create processes that assure you that you foster the best in your people.

   Perhaps you remember a time from your youth when you went bowling. The alley gutters seemed like they could reach out and snag the bowling ball. When my daughter was old enough to bowl, she showed me that with a flick of a switch, guards came out of the floor, and her bowling ball could never go off track. Processes in our organizations serve similar functions, helping our employees understand how to perform at their best, to know the boundaries within which they can work, and to protect them and our companies from significant and expensive failures.

   Without proper procedures and information, a company can fail to recognize the reasons that stand in the way of success. One of my clients faced an anemic profit picture, producing about 50% of the amount he needed to be successful in the department. He established a robust culture in his group, involving his team to find out why. I recommended the group ask the CFO and his accounting team to help to understand the root cause of the lower performance. These reports proved so valuable that their review became part of the regular departmental procedures, enabling the group to know precisely where they stand at the end of each month.

   The first review showed that 1/3 of the clients with whom the group worked were unprofitable. Fees charged to customers did not cover expenses. By taking quick action, my client was able to turn the ship around, increasing his profit by 50% the following year.

   John Weaver, who founded the Weaver Consultants Group over twenty-five years ago, explained his philosophy. Weaver Consultants Group has been profitable every year of their existence, growing to well over $100 million. John told me that a top reason for success was the creation of financial processes second to none. Every leader knows where they stand all the time. Each year, John's accounting firm releases benchmarks that enable the accounting firm's clients to compare their financial results to the very best. John's organization reaches such heights of performance that the accounting firm would not include Weaver Consultants Group's numbers in their benchmark. The accounting firm explained Weaver Consultants Group results would skew the benchmark to such a high level that others would be unable to reach it.

Tom Walter, who, with his brothers, started Tasty Catering, knows the value of procedures that help the company create a top culture and make money. In a two-story-high room where the Tasty Catering group shares a meal every day, a plastic writable surface covers one wall. Each aspect of the business, from sales to purchasing, shows up as a line item on the large plastic sheet. The entire company meets regularly and updates performance numbers against budget. When the numbers look good, everybody applauds. When the numbers don't meet budget expectations, there is silence followed by a question: "Do you need help with this line?"

Because of well-defined processes, employees know they can impact company performance and understand what decisions they can and cannot make. They feel as though the company belongs to them.

Top-notch processes help us, as leaders, to focus our employees on success and avoid straying into distractions that will lead the employee and the organization into difficulty. These boundaries bring out the best in employees and help illuminate the bright shining stars within our organizations.

Deliberate Practice for Expert Performance to Find the Bright Shining Star Within

Finding the bright shining star within everyone is really about creating a setting in which employees can find the best in themselves. You, as a leader, set up the environment that brings out the terrific talents and capabilities in your people.

1. Make a concerted effort to understand everyone's strengths. Have them work on their strengths every day.

2. Uncover and be sure that the person routinely works within the Expert Performance Success Map™ that maximizes personal performance.

3. Respect what your people do, and they will respect you and your company.

4. Build a compelling culture in which everyone can shine.

5. Create robust processes that assure everyone can become successful.

Are you ready to find the bright shining stars? Assess yourself and understand your growth opportunities at

www.expertperformance.com/find-the-stars.

CHAPTER 12

CONCLUSION

Lead with care, compassion and understanding and move your organization to breathtaking performance

I hope you will have the opportunity to practice and master many of the top leadership skills that I have presented in this book. Each chapter has provided you with secrets from the very best leaders, secrets that when used consistently, will deliver high performance for you and throughout your organization. I suggest that you review each chapter, discovering four or fewer skill areas that you want to grow. While at work, feel free to practice each skill daily for twenty to thirty days, the time our minds take to make new neural connections. By the end of this period, you will have developed new habits using these capabilities. Return to the book to uncover more skills that you would find valuable, then repeat the process. You will be amazed at how quickly you grow your expertise.

With so many things to practice, where does one start? From my corporate positions with IBM, my consulting work with top clients, and work with experts, including the hundreds of interviews I have conducted over twenty-two years, leadership begins with concern, care, and compassion, something I learned from my personal experiences.

I used to believe leadership was magical, somehow absorbed through something mystical and unknown. Leaders seem to pop up before me, fully formed, without practice or learning. I no longer believe this.

We never lead in isolation from our history, for we are an amalgam of our life experiences. Many of these experiences take us down paths that enhance our leadership capabilities, while others require reformulating and reframing to serve us in our work. At times, these life happenings jolt us with their power and send us in an unexpected direction, a direction that promotes clarity and insight.

With the entirety of my work, I have found a critical aspect of leadership. The best of leaders begin with care, compassion, and understanding. I came to this conclusion after years of conversations with the top leaders, but it wasn't until I had the experience I relate below that I realized the power of connection. Perhaps you might recall from this example pieces from your own life's journey and gain fuller insight into what has impacted you to send you down the road to become extraordinary.

Abby

In the spring of April 1996, a tiny girl child was born outside Nanning in southwest China, in a small village called Pum Yao. At that time, China forbade couples from having more than one child, so her desperate parents pinned a note with her birthday on her clothing, then left the three-day-old baby in a hospital in their village, a tiled hallway leading to a few rooms, where they knew she would be found and cared for. I cannot begin to imagine what her parents felt leaving their child behind. Even after three days, I am sure they felt a powerful bond to their newborn, and leaving her alone must have been agonizing.

Hospital workers took her in, and a few days later, the local mayor transported the baby girl to the state orphanage in Nanning, where dedicated workers did their best to care for her and a room filled with orphaned babies. The caretakers gave the child a name, Yuan Ching Ning, the last name, Yuan, means public, Ching translates to green, and Ning is peaceful. She was a quiet child who cried and fussed little—a disadvantage, for it was the babies that made the most noise who received attention. Through no fault of their own, the orphanage workers did not know that children must be held and comforted. Without human connection, children suffer trauma and can even die. (Children are not the only ones who suffer from lack of connection. I have witnessed compassionless leaders who struggle with relationship, who then stunt or even destroy their organizations.)

Ching Ning, at about twelve months, caught the attention of an employee of a global adoption organization called Holt International, who was helping Nanning workers to modernize their care. Ching Ning's medical records alarmed Xao Xao. The worst was happening. Ching Ning suffered from anemia, a symptom of undernourishment, literally starving amid food. She wasn't eating well, gaining weight, talking, or walking, and Xao Xao feared that without intervention, Ching Ning would die. She had to take action swiftly.

Fortunately, Xao Xao quickly found a foster home for Ching Ning, where she would receive loving care, regular food, and exercise in the house of kind and experienced parents. Here she was held and loved and began to flourish. After a short two months in foster care, her American parents made the trip from Chicago to China to pick up the newest member of their family.

My wife and I wanted children but were not blessed with a family, and with resignation, we put the idea behind us. Years later, the thought of family surfaced when my Dad passed away, and I felt an intense longing to be a father. I approached my wife, Barb, telling her of my awakened desires to have a child. To my surprise, she had similar thoughts and told me, coincidentally, that the Holt International adoption agency representatives were presenting locally that weekend. The event rocked us with deep emotions, convincing us to apply to adopt a child from China. A year before Ching Ning's birth, we began a long, two-year process that included training, classes, background checks, and a compilation of stacks of papers to justify to Chinese officials why we would be great parents–followed by a long wait for the Chinese government to match us with a child.

One day, a letter and a small picture arrived in the mail while I was at work. Barb called me and left a voice message with words I'll never forget: "She's beautiful." We were to leave in just a few months to adopt Ching Ning.

After a 16 hour trip to Hong Kong, and with only a few days to recover, we boarded another airplane to make the hour-long trek to the Nanning orphanage. A delayed flight brought us to our hotel after midnight, and that night, we slept fitfully, anxious about the next morning when we would meet our new daughter. The following day, a bus filled with weary parents-to-be took us to the orphanage where Ching Ning's foster mother had brought her for the adoption. Eight families met their children for the first time, and as the orphanage workers handed the babies to the strange Americans, most of the children protested and cried. Ching Ning, however, did not make a sound. She stared wide-eyed at the other babies and us as we held our daughter for the first time.

The first night, Ching Ning, now named Abby, refused to eat or sleep. All alone in a foreign hotel room, Barb struggled to calm Abby and encourage her to drink a few drops of formula. We knew that the hot, September southern-China weather would cause dehydration, and as new parents, our anxiety grew as we worried about our tiny, frail daughter, now a life who had become our full responsibility. After several hours of coaxing, Abby finally took a few swallows, causing us to feel a small sense of relief.

As the youngest in my family, I had never taken care of small children before now, let alone my own, and the obligation felt enormous, striking me hard. I thought that perhaps I had made the biggest mistake of my life until...

Abby was crawling but not yet walking. One afternoon, finally stoked with food and rest, as she crawled around the hotel room floor, I would pop out over the tops of the bed and surprise her. For such a little girl, she gave out the biggest belly laugh. For the next thirty minutes, we laughed and played.

I was in love! And have been ever since. I hadn't realized how much my parents loved me until I had a child of my own. Each time I think about it, the thought that our daughter came close to death in the orphanage fills me with grief and deep sadness.

The week felt like a whirlwind of activity, including Abby's Chinese adoption and passport processing. It was during that week that we took a trip to the hometown where Abby was left and met with the Mayor who had taken her to the orphanage. I recall the powerful emotions I felt, feelings that still vividly color the picture of that day. Through the interpretation of Xao Xao, the mayor repeated, "Lucky baby. Lucky baby." Tears welled up in Barb's, the mayor's, and my eyes. All we could manage to say was, "No, we are lucky." Tears still come as I think of that moment.

We need not have worried about Abby eating. She could not stop eating. I am sure she was making up for lost time. While still in China, this small child put away large bowls of Chinese rice and meat cereal. If we paused, even for a moment, during which I could accurately describe as an Abby feeding frenzy, she would raise a dramatic and vocal commotion, letting us know in no uncertain terms of her displeasure. Barb and I had little time to feed ourselves. We both lost weight.

Two weeks after we gathered Abby in our arms, and after another long flight from Hong Kong, we arrived home with our beautiful daughter. She was still small, about the size of a six-month-old, weighing only about 15 ½ pounds. I could wrap my hand around her thighs. She wasn't walking; she wasn't saying any words.

In that first year, I learned life's most valuable lesson – the power of love! During those early days, Abby became a different person, developing a welcoming and fun-loving personality. In the first twelve months, Abby added seven pounds to her weight, began walking, grew twelve teeth, and started saying words.

Twenty-three years later, she has blossomed into a lovely person and a conscientious, hard worker. She feels tremendous empathy for others, has studied hard, and now cares for classrooms full of young children.

Leadership, Compassion, and Caring

From the depths of my thinking, somehow I knew the power of connection, but Abby's experience brought home in a tangible, real way that care, compassion, and understanding make us thrive and blossom, no matter past circumstances. I witness this same care and compassion in the best leaders, who create incredible businesses where everyone feels a connection, ownership, and personal engagement.

I wish for you that you find in your heart to become the leader who first fills your organization with understanding, compassion, and caring. By finding expert performance in yourself and your people, you will go on to produce amazing results with the team you have!

ABOUT THE AUTHOR

Dr. Racioppo is an internationally renowned speaker and consultant who brings a wealth of experience and a high level of growth and innovation to every organization.

From his ten years of experience at IBM, Vince brings the secrets of a large, successful corporation to today's businesspeople.

As president of the Center for Expert Performance, Inc., his twenty-plus years of groundbreaking work in high performance brings a distinctive and fresh look at how leaders produce top-notch results. He has been featured in publications such as **Selling Power Magazine** and was a regular contributor to **Metal Marketplace.**

He has provided innovative programs for organizations such as Bank of America, Siemens, Jones Lang LaSalle, Mercury Marine, Motorola, Manpower, Sanford Pen, Ameritech, and Discover Card. He earned a Ph.D. from the University of Iowa.

Vince would delight in the opportunity to engage you in a conversation and join him in the journey to change the way America leads! You are personally invited to call or write with your thoughts and comments to:

847 840 9926 or email Racioppo@expertperformance.com.

Join with him on
www.linkedin.com/in/racioppo
Twitter vincer

LINKS TO SELF ASSESSMENTS

Each chapter ends with an opportunity for you to assess your leadership behaviors and expertise. Here are the links:

Chapter 2 www.expertperformance.com/hire-the-best

Chapter 3 www.expertperformance.com/train-for-success

Chapter 4 www.expertperformance.com/engage-and-grow

Chapter 5 www.expertperformance.com/power-of-strengths

Chapter 6 www.expertperformance.com/be-more-profitable

Chapter 7 www.expertperformance.com/Leading-leaders

Chapter 8 www.expertperformance.com/power-of-influence

Chapter 9 www.expertperformance.com/get-top-performance

Chapter 10 www.expertperformance.com/build-an-expert-team

Chapter 11 www.expertperformance.com/find-the-stars

APPENDIX

Useful Charts and Examples

Chapter Two

Essential elements of a job description

- **Tasks** – Tasks are the core of a job description, allowing us to specify the duties and activities a person must perform. Generally, most organizations get this right about 80 to 90% of the time. We can fail to produce an adequate task list if we do not understand the job. For example, we may not understand higher-level positions such as controllers or executives, and we, therefore, fail to capture the nuances of these jobs. To obtain the details of positions may require observation of either incumbents or of those performing a similar function.

- **Knowledge** – Candidates must have a minimal level of job knowledge. If we have to teach our new hires the basics, but we don't have the resources to do so, we put the outcomes of the organization in jeopardy.

- **Skills** – Successful candidates must have necessary skill levels, such as the ability to make complex calculations or use a spreadsheet. Ordinarily, organizations are quite good at specifying the required skills and knowledge.

- **Experience** – The experience of the candidate may add significant reasons for success. Experience, as in on-the-job training, brings individuals a leg up on those who have limited time in the position. Many organizations specify the number of years of experience. I have found these to be somewhat arbitrary and do not recommend you use an exact number as a filter for identifying unqualified candidates. Two years of experience in a major accounting firm may have a far more significant impact than two years at a small, boutique company.

I have observed two common errors when defining knowledge, skills, and experience.

The first error is a lack of clear understanding of the knowledge, skills, and experience necessary to do the job. This error is more likely to occur when the individual who is hiring has not performed in the position.

The second and more common error occurs when our budgets prevent us from hiring a person of sufficient competency levels.

One of my clients had to hire four new individuals for his department. His performance plan requires him to maintain a 70% billable rate in the consulting firm, i.e., he needs to bill 70% of his time to clients. Unfortunately, the four people he hired, through no fault of their own, were not up to full competency level for the job. He, therefore, had to spend much of his time teaching and training, and, consequently, his billable rate fell to 50%.

He was expected to make up that 20% difference by working extra hours. Such overtime hours can lead to fatigue, burnout, and attrition. Unfortunately, the majority of organizations failed to capture the cost of developing and training people to full capability levels.

- **Cultural fit** – As you know, every organization has a distinctive culture. During my days in IBM, when we hired someone who functioned outside our culture, the organizational immune system activated, and the individual realizing the bad fit departed quickly. Strong cultures can have a profound effect on how well an individual performs.

  We think of culture as having three components that are all necessary for an organization's high performance. First, the culture has to focus on high customer satisfaction levels with people in the organization feeling driven to exceed customer needs. Second, the organization must establish a highly focused effort to engage employees. In high-performing cultures, these employees willingly bring discretionary effort to the workplace, offering their talents, thoughts, and creativity to advance the organization. Third, organizations must have tight financial controls. The most effective organizations we see are those that share financial information with their employees, creating a sense of camaraderie and collaboration as these employees work to reach business goals.

- **Learning ability** – Our research tells us that our ability to learn is one of the single most significant factors that contribute to an individual's work success. I am reminded of an individual who I helped to hire at a company with whom I was working. Others liked this individual, and we believed he had all the characteristics necessary to perform at a high level. Unfortunately, the individual could not work with spreadsheets, a critical component of his job. Even after multiple interventions and training, he remained unable to master these essential tools. As a result, the company was forced to let this individual go.

- **Ability to work in a team** – More and more, work funnels through teams who often out-produce individual effort. Organizations continue to drive out bureaucracy and, with that, layers of management. Companies no longer can afford to have top-down, command-and-control leadership since many individuals in today's workforce will not tolerate this kind of leadership.

- **Emotional intelligence** – Our ability to work cooperatively with and influence others has a profound impact on the success of our organization. Emotional intelligence predicts success in the workplace, particularly as leaders ascend in their careers. Interestingly, in opposition to cognitive intelligence, emotional intelligence can be learned and continues to grow into our 60s, when most people retire from their organizations. When hiring, we can screen for emotional intelligence with the understanding that those who score less than competency level can be developed and trained to increase their EI. I use the EQ-I 2.0 and EQ 360, which can be found at www.mhs.com (look under talent offerings).

Sample Job Description with Onboarding and Development Costs

	Detailed description of minimal competency for hiring	Detailed description when at a competency level	How will the person be brought up to competency level	Estimated cost description	
Knowledge	Has completed the coursework for an accounting degree	Knowledge of our internal accounting practices	Will connect individual to a senior accountant who will teach the required practices.	120 hours of senior accountants time over one year	$6,000
Skills	Must know how to use Excel basics	Must be able to create Pivot tables from raw data, including averages and sums.	Will send the individual to course on Excel. Will have the individual use Excel Pivotables.	Excel course and work with senior accountant	$500
Experience	One year working at a 100-person-or-more accounting firm	One additional year working at our firm	Teach the following: 1) How to conduct a month-end closing. 2) Produce job-costing reports for your assigned team.	Lowered productivity calculated at 1/3 salary	$20,000
Cultural Fit	Has worked in teams in previous jobs and college. Is assertive but not demanding.	Has excellent client service. Understands company financials. Works well within our teams.	Learn the mission and vision of our organization. Place on an internal team. Review company financials with the individual.	Lowered productivity of internal team	10,000
Learning Ability	Has an IQ of at least 110. Has a drive to learn new things.	n/a	n/a	n/a	n/a
Ability to work in a team	Treats all people with dignity and respect.	Treats all people with dignity and respect. Willing to do what is necessary to get the job done, i.e. has drive.	Teach about drive and expectations for performance.	Included above	Included above

Emotional Intelligence	Scores in the top 20% of emotional intelligence instruments	Scores in top 10% of emotional intelligence instruments	Develop emotional intelligence through use of online learning.	Subscription to online emotional intelligence learning	500
Investment to bring person to competency level					$37,000

Chapter 3 – Train for Success

Deficit versus Appreciative Coaching Example

Deficit Coaching Conversation (how not to do coaching)

Coach: Marie, I understand from your manager that you are having some challenges in communicating with your colleagues. I know that they comment that you are sometimes short with them.

Marie: I want to get things done, and sometimes my colleagues ask the same questions over and over again.

Coach: Marie, perhaps we can fix this problem by helping you learn listening techniques.

Marie: I think I'm a pretty good listener already. I'm not sure that you could teach me anything that I don't already have a handle on.

Coach: Well, you may not have learned these listening techniques that I offer.

Marie: I've been through about three or four listening classes.

Coach: I think you will find my approach different than others.

Marie: Everyone says I'm a good listener. I don't think you're listening to me.

By now, I think you understand that the conversation is going badly, and Marie is becoming more and more resistant. I realized that deficit coaching tends to cause people to be on guard and on edge. By using an appreciative approach, I was able to overcome resistance and use it to help my clients.

Appreciative Coaching

Coach: Marie, I understand that you have great strengths, and your boss would like you to be even stronger than you are today.

Marie: Yes, I think I do a pretty good job, although sometimes I think I irritate people.

Coach: Help me understand how you think you sometimes irritate people.

Marie: I want to get things done, and sometimes people ask the same questions over and over again.

Coach: I'm sure that it can be annoying to you. Does it slow you down?

Marie: You are exactly on target. I want to get my work done, and these repetitive questions distract me.

Coach: You have some terrific strengths helping you to perform at a high level. Wouldn't it be great if everyone performed at that level?

Marie: It sure would. But how do I get those around me to pay more attention and work faster?

Chapter 4 – Engage and Grow Your Employees

Essential elements to grow engagement.

- **Assure that your organization's mission and vision are apparent, easily remembered, and compelling.**

- **Make development planning for your employees an inseparable part of your culture.**

- **Set clear expectations for performance.**

- **Hire and develop great leaders who care about and listen to their people.**

Chapter 6 – Be More Profitable

Example Profitability Report

Duckling Imprints	20%
NoGo Taxi	18%
Make No Sense Analytics	17%
LZ E Service	17%
Poors Design	17%
Lobster Bisque Co	17%
Bobs Boxing Square	16%
Knotty Carpentry	15%
Flips 2 Day Plumbing Service	15%
XYZ Alphabet Lettering	15%
Long Time Waite Medical	13%
Madison Square Gardening	11%
Flambeau Field Athletics	10%
Faul Threw Roofing	6%
Left Feet Dance Studio	5%
Self Repair Auto	-4%
Waterless Car Wash	-5%
Left Over Foods	-7%

Profit by Person

Amber T Topsales	$85,002
Larry No'Two	$77,312
Ella M. Good	$74,899
Sam T Middleman	$50,189
Manford Halfway	$45,000
Mila Beelow	$15,200
Languid Seller	$1,159
Laston List	-$32,000

Chapter 7 – Leading Leaders

Professional Delegation

1. **Create Clarity** - The more precise information we as leaders provide, the more likely we will receive what we want from the person to whom we have delegated tasks. Clarity offers a complete understanding of how we know the person to whom we have delegated tasks will be successful.

2. **Provide clear end dates. Add check-in conversations if needed.**

   Providing a precise due date and time not only ensures success, but such a practice also enables leadership to balance workloads. Once you've assigned a date and time, record the information in your calendar. Doing so helps in two ways. First, you can easily hold folks accountable to the end dates, and second, you can effortlessly discern whether you have assigned too many tasks to one person.

3. Hold each other accountable.

   To round out one's ability to delegate effectively, you will want to hold religiously to your negotiated end dates. As I mentioned earlier, the best managers will write check-in and end dates on their calendar, then immediately follow up when the manager does not meet expectations. This follow-up educates your staff that dues dates are serious.

Chapter 8 – The Power Of Influence

Six Critical Elements to Building Trust

1. Frequent use of reflective language

2. Regular practice of empathic language

3. Framing of issues

4. The reframing of tough or challenging problems

5. Embracing and using defensiveness of others

6. Ability to give negative feedback.

Reflective Language Examples

Example 1

Other person: I had a run-in with my boss today. She was in a foul mood and just seemed as though she could not listen to me.

You: You had a run-in with your boss today? (By using their words, you have let the other person know that you are listening.)

Example 2

Other person: I am upset with the way you've handled this sale to our company.

You: if I understand correctly, you are upset with the way with I handled the sale to your company. Tell me more so that I can understand what happened. (You have let the person know that you are listening as well as demonstrating care for the other person's perceptions. This technique is an excellent way to reduce conflict.)

Example 3 – How NOT to do reflective listening

Other person: I had a run-in with my boss today. She was in a foul mood and just seemed as though she could not listen.

You: I suggest you go back in to tell your boss that she needs to take a minute to listen to you. (Probably the biggest listening mistake most of us make is trying to solve the other person's problem. Most of us can solve our problems once we feel calm. A calm state of mind releases the resources to address those challenges.)

Empathic Language Examples

Other person: I had a run-in with my boss today. She was in a foul mood and just seemed as though she could not listen to me.

You: You had a run-in with your boss today? I'm sorry to hear that. Seems like she was in a foul mood. (This is an example of two reflective language statements.)

Other person: Yes, I had terrific ideas that she dismissed.

You: So in addition to not listening to you, she dismissed your ideas (two more examples of reflective listening).

Other person: Yeah, I got out of there as fast as I could. That'll be about the last time I bring new ideas to her.

You: That whole situation must have been pretty annoying, and from what you've told me, you were pretty ticked. (This is the first opportunity to use empathic language–annoying and ticked).

Other person: Yep, I was pretty angry about the situation (the person has opened up to precisely how they felt–angry).

Empathic language provides an excellent opportunity to demonstrate that you not only heard what was said, you also exhibit compassion and caring. Such behavior will help you to enhance your connection to the other person.

Framing Examples – Wrong and Right Way

Wrong Way:

Owner: Jim, your performance has not been at a level we find acceptable. In fact, your work is pretty average. We want you to take a couple of assessments to find out where your challenges are and see if we can correct them.

Employee: I had no idea you were dissatisfied.

Owner: Now you know.

Here is the right way to frame. (I told my client to take the following approach.)

Owner: Jim, we value you here and want to invest in your success. I have a colleague and friend who is an excellent coach, and we would like you to work with him. Your success is as vital to us as it is to you. He'll send you several links to assessments, and then we'll understand what your most substantial capabilities are and how we can maximize those.

Employee: That sounds terrific. There are several areas in which I feel like I could use the help. Let's get started.

Reframing Example

Linda: I spent all evening completing the Baker report because I thought our boss needed it at 8 o'clock this morning. When I arrived at 7:30, she told me that, last night, the meeting had been postponed until tomorrow. That sure is annoying since I worked so hard.

You: (Begin with reflective and empathic language.) Wow, you spent all evening getting ready for a meeting that's not happening until tomorrow. I can see how annoyed you are since she knew last night that the meeting had been postponed.

Linda: Yes, I wish she would've called.

You: That sure would've been nice had she called. Well, (here's the reframe) at least your work is done, and the report is complete. You can take that off your mind and do something that is more productive.

Linda: Yes, I wish she would've called, but you are right. At least the report is complete.

Stop Fighting Resistance

Here are the steps:	Example:
Use reflective listening to let the other person know you understand.	You: I know you will be an excellent leader and make a difference in this organization. I think you need to step up and take the role. Other person: I'm not so sure that I can do this. You: So you're not sure that you can step up to the new role?
Employ empathic listening to deepen the connection so that the other person feels less confrontational and more engaged in your conversation.	Other person: Yes, that's correct. I've been able to run my practice, but that's different than running the entire division. You: From what you're saying, you seem to be a bit concerned about taking a bigger leadership role. Other person: Yes, I don't know if I can do it.

Make sure that you understand the issue.	You: What stands in your way? Other person: I've never done a role like this before, and the previous leader had such an impact. I'm not sure I can fill her shoes.
Help the individual discover resources in other aspects of his or her life that can be used in the current situation.	You: I want you to think about times when you were asked to lead other groups in your past. Other person: Well, I've been asked to lead just about every organization I've been in. In college, I was asked to be the president of my sorority. All through my work, people asked me to lead different efforts. You: If I understand you correctly, you have been asked to run many different organizations and efforts. Is that correct? Other person: Yes, that's correct. You: Have you been successful in these engagements? If so, how did you know what to do? Other person: Well, I used to make a list before I started the new job of all the things that I needed to accomplish and know. I would start working on that list right away.
Help the person use the new resource in the current situation.	You: What if you were to do the same process in this situation? Make your list and begin to discover what you need to know and learn. Other person: Yes, that makes a lot of sense. I think I could get started on this right away.

Appeal to the Motivations of Others

Steps	Example
Ask the person, "What is important to you personally in your work?"	Other person: It's important to me to please the customer.
Ask, "What else is personally important to you and your work?"	Other person: I like to be accurate.
Continue asking, "What else is important to you personally in your work?" until the person repeats or ends.	Other person: I think that's about it.

Ask, "If you have all those things that you mentioned, what will they do for you?" (You are listening for big concept words like satisfaction, fulfillment, or enjoyment.)	Other person: I feel satisfied.
If you have a project or an activity which you want the other person to engage in, you can tie the activity back to the other person's motivation.	You: I have a project that will please a lot of customers. Would you be interested in participating? (Because the person had mentioned the importance of pleasing customers, we tie the project directly back to the individual's motivation.)

Elements of Flawless Execution

1. Use of specific language
2. Positive language
3. Future-paced language
4. Removing barriers

Specific Language Example

(How not to communicate using specific language) You need to communicate more effectively.	This phrase has at least two unspecified words. The first and most apparent is *communicate*, and the second is *effectively*. Neither term tells us precisely what we need to do.
(An example of specific language) I need you to communicate in a way that lets me know how you are spending your work time. I need to know the projects you are working on and the time spent on each. Please give me this information verbally each Monday at 4 o'clock.	These sentences provide a precise instruction set. Notice the clarity and specificity.

Positive Language Example

Negative example	Positive example
I notice you are frequently late for work.	I would like you to work very hard to come in on time to the office.
Your communication skills are lacking.	Let's work together to grow your communication skills.
Please stop complaining and do your job.	I want to hear your concerns as well as watch you excel at your job.

Future Language Example

Past: You made a mistake with the client by disagreeing with his request.	Future: I would like to offer several thoughts on how you might handle clients who disagree with you.
Past: You missed your quota last year.	Future: This year, you'll reach your quota. We'll work together to make that happen.

Making Other's Jobs Easier – Right and Wrong Example

You: I need the budget forecast for the new account by Friday.	Other: I'll get it to you.
Monday arrives. You: It's Monday and I still don't have the analysis.	Other: Sorry I didn't get it to you. I had trouble locating the spreadsheet template we use. Then I had difficulty finding the data. In the middle of the project with you, my boss gave me a short assignment. I'll get it to you by day's end.
Here is a better way:	
You: (You will want to send an email and follow with a phone confirmation.) The customer asked me for a budget forecast for their board meeting on the following Tuesday, so I need to get the report from you by Friday. You can find the template you will need on the D drive in the analytics folder. It is titled Budget Forecast. You can get the data from the lead salesperson. He put the original plans together and has a spreadsheet. Are you available Wednesday for a check-in to find out if you have any questions or challenges? Feel free to call me any time.	Other: Thanks for the information and location of the data. That helps. I'll check with my boss to learn whether we have any upcoming projects. Wednesday at 9 am is an excellent time for a status report. I hope that works for you. I'll keep you posted.

Monday arrives. You: Thank you for getting the report to me on Friday. It is great, as usual. You always do terrific work.	Other: You made it easy by helping me understand deadlines as well as to locate the tools and information I needed. Our boss asked me to do a small project, but when I explained the situation, he said I could work on it after I completed the forecast for you.

Conflict Resolution Example

First, seek to understand (see reflective and empathic language). Validate the other person's concerns.	Other: I want to work from home. Other companies do that. It would make a difference for me. You: If I understand, you want to work from home since others do that. Doing so will make a difference. Am I correct? Other: Yes, that's right.
Understand the person's motivations.	You: What's important to you about working from home? Other: I have a long commute and spending more time with my family is a priority. You: I understand. Your family time is important.
Respectfully explain your position.	You: At this time, we have no policies that allow people to work at home. Other: I see. Are there any exceptions?
Determine your conflict style. Compromise or Collaboration is often the most effective. Sometimes competitive is necessary when you cannot break the rules.	
Build an agreement frame. An agreement frame works particularly well with both the compromise and collaboration styles. Agreement frames seek to help the other person achieve what is important to him or her while still holding to what we value.	You: I would like to find a way to help you spend more time with your family while meeting the needs of our company. If I could find a way to help you, would you be willing to help us? Other: Yes, I would. You: In talking to HR, they are afraid of setting a precedent which would allow individuals to work at home. You are a highly valued employee. Since you would like to spend more time with your family, we would like to offer you a flexible start time so that you may spend more time at home in the morning or evening. With this work for you? Other: I know this is not ideal for me, but it sure helps me spend more time with my family when I need to. Thank you.

Appreciation Examples

What you notice	**What you say**
You notice the other person regularly helps others after she completes her work.	"I appreciate how you are always willing to help others. You are a helpful person."
You notice the other person has a cheery disposition.	"I appreciate how you are always so upbeat. Having you around makes us all feel better."
You notice the other person can quickly create spreadsheets.	"I appreciate how quickly you can create a spreadsheet. You are very good at that."

Direct and Indirect Speech

What	When to Use	Example
Level 1. Command - has no deference or indirect language	A command is particularly valuable when there is an urgent need to take action.	"Finish this report by 5 o'clock, or we will lose this customer."
Level 2. Team Obligation Statement – is inclusive of the whole team	When we want to create collaboration, we use a team obligation statement.	"Let's all work together to finish this report by 5 o'clock."
Level 3. Team Suggestion – uses a question to enhance inclusivity	Use the team suggestion to create inclusion while speaking in a less direct way.	"Why don't we all work together to see if we can finish this report by 5 o'clock?"
Level 4. Query – questioning used to be more indirect	One can use a question to prompt a group to think in a specific direction.	"Do you think it would be helpful for us to get the report done by 5 o'clock?"
Level 5. Preference – a statement used indirectly to specify a bias	We use preference statements to guide the group down a particular path.	"Perhaps we should look at different ways we can organize to get the report done."
Level 6. Hint – the most indirect form of mitigated speech	When you want to plant an idea without specifying the idea. Sometimes used to avoid conflict.	"I wonder if we have any important deadlines we should reach today."

Openness Example

Situation	How Not to Be Open	How to Be Open
You forgot to complete a task for a friend at work.	I was so busy I couldn't get to your task.	I'm sorry. I completely forgot. It's my fault.
You can't create a spreadsheet that you need for a project.	It's not my fault. I was never trained to use spreadsheets this way.	I don't know how to create this spread-sheet. I need help.
You didn't make your quota for the month.	There were too many things out of my con-trol that prevented me from reaching quota.	Even though there were a lot of things out of my control, it's still my responsibility to reach quota. I should've asked for help.
Customers are complain-ing because of late orders.	I can't be held respon-sible if customers are calling to complain at 10 o'clock at night.	I totally missed this one. I need to check the logs to find out if customers are complaining late at night.
A beloved colleague is critically ill.	He will be okay. There's nothing to worry about.	This is very hard. I'm very concerned about our friend. I wish there were something I could do to make it better.

Chapter 9 – How to Get Top Performance

Step One – Identify Your Experts

Selection Criteria (use any com-bination of the items below)	**Sales Example**
Your experts will consistently produce at the top 10% of all employees over a 3 to 5 year.	You want to find those who are at the top 10% of sales.
Experts will be identified as top people by a group of leaders.	Ask your leaders who they think their top people are. Rather than look at sales only, use other crite-ria such as attitude and drive.
Experts have influence and made a pos-itive impact beyond their departments.	Look for salespeople who have led committees, mentored others, or have innovated across the company.
Peers and others recognize these people as leaders.	Find those individuals who are mentioned by others as leaders and top performers.

Produce an Expert Performance Success Map™

Questions to ask to produce the Expert Performance Success Map™	Example Expert Performance Superintendent Success Map™ of a field superintendent at an example company – leads electrical construction projects
1. Beliefs and Motivations: What is important to you personally in your work? (This is a motivation and beliefs question that taps into a person's primary beliefs. Usually, individuals will have no more than 4 to 6 responses.)	1. (Coaches and Mentors Others) I find it important to move each person through a process from one area of expertise to another as each skill is mastered. 2. (Communicates effectively) It's important to communicate well with the team, vendors, and contractors. No misunderstandings. I handle conflicts before they can become destructive. 3. (Financial Acumen) Superintendents must understand the financials of a project. 4. (Lead) I believe in the importance of clear outcomes, which we should achieve through people who we have grown and developed.
2. Evidence: Thinking about how you answered question one, how do you know you have each one of the items? (This question asks for evidence. What do we notice when we have successfully implemented our motivations and beliefs?)	1. Everyone has a one-on-one development relationship with a leader or supervisor. 2. I notice few misunderstandings. We address conflict quickly and without blow-ups 3. Through the superintendent, everyone understands where projects are financially. 4. Goals and outcomes have been clearly stated. Everyone knows what these goals are and are working toward them.
3. Strategies: Again thinking about how you answered question one, let's walk through each item and understand the strategies you use to fulfill your beliefs and motivations. (By tapping into strategies, we fully understand how an individual achieves the results they want.)	Because strategies may have considerable detail, I have shown a sample below in a separate table. Each strategy corresponds to a belief or motivation mentioned in step 1 above.

Sample Strategies for an Expert Performance Success Map™

1. Coaches and Mentors

I have weekly conversations with each employee to help them grow and develop.

I give regular feedback to my people almost daily to help them overcome problems and get better at their work.

I assign progressively more difficult projects to each employee so that they can grow and develop.

I show by example what it takes to produce good work.

I have a plan in mind for each person to grow and develop them.

I continually think of ways to prepare my people so I can help promote my employees to higher levels in the organization.

I become the learner in a mentoring situation so that I can understand the person I am mentoring.

2. Effectively Communicates

When I influence, I make sure that I understand the other person's motivations.

I take time to listen so that I fully understand what the person is saying.

I have regular meetings between the field and general contractors to be assured that we are all communicating clearly with one another.

I address conflict head-on and make sure that it doesn't get hurtful.

If I have a conflict with a general contractor, I call a meeting to address it as soon as possible.

I hold regular meetings with the team so that everybody understands not only the status of the project but what is happening in the organization as a whole.

3. Financial Acumen

I know where my projects are almost daily financially—at least weekly.

I take courses at my company to understand the financials of the company.

I teach others how to manage the finances of a project.

I stay on top of billings, making sure that they are put out timely and paid.

I make everyone financially responsible for their part of the project.

4. Lead

I share expectations upfront so the team can achieve.
Goals are team goals and are communicated that way.
"Meets" is unacceptable–I help the team strategize for "Exceeds" level.
I promote competition, comparing results with other teams.
I gather and use performance measurements.
I make sure everyone feels empowered to solve problems.
I allow people to make mistakes as long as they don't put the project significantly in danger.
I make sure people feel that they have responsibility for the job and feel connected to it.

Example Expert Performance Success Map™ Benchmark

Coaches and Mentors	Creates a work environment that maximizes people's growth and development.
	Helps the team grow the skills necessary to produce project outcomes.
	Provides promotion opportunities.
	Demonstrates an example of hard work.
Effectively Communicates	When influencing, connects desired outcomes to the other person's motivation.
	Listens well.
	Works to create open communication between operations, field, vendors, GC's, and owners to assure efficiency and profitability.
	Continuously communicates with the team through activities such as daily meetings.
	Brings up issues even at the risk of conflict or discomfort.
Manages Finances	Runs a financially successful project, including budgets and margins.
	Monitors how money is being spent in the project, assuring a profitable outcome.
	Understands how to read financial reports for a project.
	Manages billings effectively.

Leads Effectively	Holds everyone to high standards of performance.
	Gives freedom to people to make decisions while functioning on their own.
	Is not punitive when individuals make mistakes.
	Encourages employees to take responsibility for major portions of a project.
	Helps employees to feel empowered to solve their own problems, not accepting excuses.
	Helps individuals feel connected to and responsible for the job.

Chapter 10 - Build an Expert Performance Team

Six critical steps for building an expert performance team:

1. Focus on positivity and the future.
2. Build openness and trust.
3. Foster amazing decision-making.
4. Make decisions stick.
5. Hold each other responsible.
6. Focus on outcomes.

Example Focus on Positivity

Traditional Leadership	Positive and Future Expert Leadership
It's crucial that we hit our goals for this year so that we may have enough cash flow to run our operations. We made a lot of mistakes over the last six months, and we can't afford to repeat these.	I am feeling so confident that we will reach our goals this year, helping us to make our organization stronger and providing more rewards to you as a company associate. Over the last year, we hit a few speed bumps, and I know we have learned much that will be valuable for reaching our goals.

Build Openness and Trust

Steps	Examples
1. Focus on the need for two groups as one team pursuing the same results.	"Your team serves a higher purpose, both to one another and to the entire organization. If your team were wildly successful, what goals would your team reach? What would be your role?"
2. Offer exercises and activities that allow individuals to open up.	"Sometimes working on a team can be challenging. Think about your team in the future. If the future were marvelous, what would change? What would you change personally?" Here's another excellent question. "What has been the most challenging time in your work career and how did you overcome it?"

Foster Amazing Decision Making

Steps for Better Decision Making
Assure that everyone is heard. By deliberately calling on every team member, even those who are introverted and may not speak out, we assure ourselves of having wide-ranging input. Ask where each person stands on the pending decision.
Encourage your team to dig deep into each person's thinking, exploring every corner of an idea.
When exploring an idea, use math calculations as often as possible, when applicable. For example, many marketing and sales decisions hide hidden costs that reduce profitability.

Make Decision Stick

Steps to Make Decisions Stick
As in the previous step, be sure that everyone participates in an opportunity to express themselves.
Make the decision clear and precise. Explain what you all agree to do and by when. Use precision language, i.e., the language of the senses. What will you notice when you have committed to the decision? What will you hear, feel, see, touch, taste, or smell?
Ask every person in the group if they have any concerns about the decision that was just made. Again, every person wants to be heard.

Hold Each Other Responsible

How to hold each other responsible
With the group, define acceptable behaviors such as arriving on time for meetings, completing assignments for the group, avoiding the use of electronics, etc.
The leader must make a public commitment to the desired behaviors.
As the leader, you must hold people responsible for the desired behaviors; otherwise, no one will. Other members of the team will assume the behaviors are ok.
Periodically review behaviors that the team finds helpful and those they find distracting.

Focus on Outcomes

Steps	Example
1. Help team members realize the concerns that their fellow associates might have.	I worked with both teams to understand the positions of both the XYZ company and FinanceCo team members. Once fully exposed, the outcome for each group seemed reasonable to the other group.
2. Emphasize and focus on a broader and more encompassing outcome that creates a win-win for all parties. Enable team participants to understand that they could advance themselves while ensuring that their colleagues reach their desired results.	I helped the teams realize they had a common desire to help FinanceCo IT customers to be more successful. Doing so would also ensure job stability, contribution, and improved efficiencies.
3. Cement in place the idea that multiple groups are one team.	Working with both groups, we established the idea that we were one team, an idea that helped the team to see both groups as one instead of multiple identities.

Chapter 11 – Find the Bright Shining Stars

Five Ways to Find the Bright Shining Stars

1. Understand a person's strengths and have them work on these every day.

2. Know what patterns make a person successful.

Example Pattern

Expert Performance Success Map™	**Current Position**
Works with a sales team who identify prospects, then he can secure contracts with "warm" prospects.	He has no sales team. He has to identify prospects independently. He does not know methods to find new clients.
Able to secure contracts with identified prospects.	Can sell a contract only if the prospect is a warm lead.
Had a colleague to perform calculations which helped Max to stay caught up. Max would then check the computations.	He has to do his calculations manually and does not know the new software. Without help, Max falls behind on revenue production.
Max would delegate some of the project management activities to an intern or direct report.	Max has no direct reports or interns and must perform all project management.

3. Offer respect for what your people do.
4. Build a compelling culture in which everyone can shine.
5. Create processes that assure you that you foster the best in your people.

REFERENCES

Beck, R. a. (2015, April 21). Retrieved from https://news.gallup.com: https://news.gallup.com/businessjournal/182792/managers-account-variance-employee-engagement.aspx

Crabtree, S. (2013, October 8). *Worldwide, 13% of Employees Are Engaged at Work*. Retrieved from https://news.gallup.com: https://news.gallup.com/poll/165269/worldwide-employees-engaged-work.aspx

Herzberg, F. (2002). One More Time: How Do You Motivate Employees. *HBR On Point*, 6.

Seligman, M. M. (1979). Alleviation of Learned Helplessness in the Dog. *Psychopathology in Animal Life*, 401 – 409.

REVIEWS

"*Expert Performance: Achieve Extraordinary Results with the Team You Have -- Guaranteed!* by Vincent Racioppo made a vivid impression. I have been a business owner for over 40 years that include multiple startups – and some failures. Racioppo addresses, without his knowledge, the "why" of my failures. Simply put...one of the best business books in my reading history. The opening of the book addresses the conundrum of hiring, interviewing, screening and onboarding in a simplistic and accurate way. He relays academic theories with practical real-life stories that describe application. The chapter titled "Build an Expert Performance Team" contains the elements of Organizational Behavior applied in an understandable fashion. It is an engaging read, and one that will benefit all leaders."

Tom Walter, Owner and Chief Cultural Officer, Tasty Catering

"Read this book immediately! In his powerful new book, Vince Racioppo will help you to instantly be more successful as a leader, and make your team ten times more effective."

Sarah Victory, best-selling author and award winning speaker, President, Victory Company

"Fantastic read!!! Full of great ideas to identify your organization's "Powerful Purpose" and to develop your team."

Jeff Young, Co-President, Weaver Consultants Group

"I've read lots of books on leadership and *Expert Performance* is one of the best! In this powerful book, Dr. Racioppo describes numerous leadership challenges. For each challenge, he offers practical action steps and rich stories guaranteed to enhance human performance. If you are a leader, or are hoping to be a leader, be sure to make this book part of your library."

Olivia Parr-Rud, MS, Expert Data Scientist, Corporate Love Ambassador, Self-Love Advocate, Olivia Group

"I'm grateful for the opportunity to have read Dr. Racioppo's book and have benefited greatly from the insights on leadership offered within its pages. I found particularly beneficial how Vince was able to weave together examples of effective leadership observed from his diverse and extensive client base and past history. Whether you are leading a small project team or a large corporation, there are insights and practical leadership skills that will bring a new perspective on your historical approach to leadership."

Douglas Dorgan, Co-President, Weaver Consultants Group

"Do you want to lead with appreciation and compassion? Would you like to have a team of experts who are top performers? Look no further than this book! In his powerful book, *Expert Performance*, Dr. Vince Racioppo provides us with critically important information and tools that truly elevate team members and, ultimately, entire organizations. When it comes to understanding what motivates and inspires your most valuable resource, your team, this book is your go-to guide. *Expert Performance* is packed with best-in-class strategies that you can use for positive results right away. After reading this book, you will have the tools to enhance and build your team to achieve and maintain top performance. With *Expert Performance* by your side, you will build a compelling culture where everyone wins-- with compassion, with care, and with confidence."

Wendy Benson, CEO, 2x2 Health: Private Health Concierge, Co-Author of The Confident Patient

"Vince has created a rich blend of leadership development and coaching experience supported by a vast array of tools and activities to take the guesswork out of becoming a top-notch leader. He gives us much to ponder and to bring into our lives to become a leader that is not afraid to use the feminine qualities of leadership to bring heart into the workplace. This book is truly interactive and insightful for us all."

Linda F. Patten, Leadership Trainer for Women Entrepreneurs and Changemakers
President &CEO, Dare2Lead With Linda

Made in the USA
Monee, IL
04 February 2020

21261396R00105